S E R I E S

A NavPress Bible study on the book of

HEBREWS

NAVPRESS

A MINISTRY OF THE NAVIGATORS
P.O. BOX 35001, COLORADO SPRINGS, COLORADO 80935

The Navigators is an international Christian organization. Our mission is to reach, disciple, and equip people to know Christ and to make Him known through successive generations. We envision multitudes of diverse people in the United States and every other nation who have a passionate love for Christ, live a lifestyle of sharing Christ's love, and multiply spiritual laborers among those without Christ.

NavPress is the publishing ministry of The Navigators. NavPress publications help believers learn biblical truth and apply what they learn to their lives and ministries. Our mission is to stimulate spiritual formation among our readers.

Most Scripture quotations are from the *Holy Bible: New International Version* (NIV). Copyright © 1973, 1978, 1984, International Bible Society. Used by permission of Zondervan Bible Publishers. Other versions used are the *New American Standard Bible* (NASB), © The Lockman Foundation 1960, 1962, 1963, 1968, 1971, 1972, 1973, 1975, 1977; the *Revised Standard Version of the Bible* (RSV), copyrighted 1946, 1952, 1971, by the Division of Christian Education of the National Council of the Churches of Christ in the USA, used by permission, all rights reserved; *The New English Bible* (NEB), © The Delegates of the Oxford University Press and the Syndics of the Cambridge University Press 1961, 1970 reprinted by permission; and the *King James Version* (KJV).

Printed in the United States of America

14 15 16 17 18 19 20 / 99

FOR A FREE CATALOG OF
NAVPRESS BOOKS & BIBLE STUDIES,
CALL 1-800-366-7788 (USA)
or 1-416-499-4615 (CANADA)

CONTENTS

ACKNOWLEDGMENTS

The LIFECHANGE series has been produced through the coordinated efforts of a team of Navigator Bible study developers and NavPress editorial staff, along with a nationwide network of fieldtesters.

AUTHOR: RON RHODES
SERIES EDITOR: KAREN LEE-THORP

HOW TO USE THIS STUDY

Objectives

Most guides in the LIFECHANGE series of Bible studies cover one book of the Bible. Although the LIFECHANGE guides vary with the books they explore, they share some common goals:

1. To provide you with a firm foundation of understanding and a thirst to return to the book;
2. To teach you by example how to study a book of the Bible without structured guides;
3. To give you all the historical background, word definitions, and explanatory notes you need, so that your only other reference is the Bible;
4. To help you grasp the message of the book as a whole;
5. To teach you how to let God's Word transform you into Christ's image.

Each lesson in this study is designed to take 60 to 90 minutes to complete on your own. The guide is based on the assumption that you are completing one lesson per week, but if time is limited you can do half a lesson per week or whatever amount allows you to be thorough.

Flexibility

LIFECHANGE guides are flexible, allowing you to adjust the quantity and depth of your study to meet your individual needs. The guide offers many optional questions in addition to the regular numbered questions. The optional questions, which appear in the margins of the study pages, include the following:

Optional Application. Nearly all application questions are optional; we hope you will do as many as you can without overcommitting yourself.

For Thought and Discussion. Beginning Bible students should be able to handle these, but even advanced students need to think about them. These questions frequently deal with ethical issues and other biblical principles. They often offer cross-references to spark thought, but the references do not give

5

obvious answers. They are good for group discussions.

For Further Study. These include: a) cross-references that shed light on a topic the book discusses, and b) questions that delve deeper into the passage. You can omit them to shorten a lesson without missing a major point of the passage.

If you are meeting in a group, decide together which optional questions to prepare for each lesson, and how much of the lesson you will cover at the next meeting. Normally, the group leader should make this decision, but you might let each member choose his or her own application questions.

As you grow in your walk with God, you will find the LIFECHANGE guide growing with you—a helpful reference on a topic, a continuing challenge for application, a source of questions for many levels of growth.

Overview and Details

The study begins with an overview of Hebrews. The key to interpretation is context—what is the whole passage or book *about*?—and the key to context is purpose—what is the author's *aim* for the whole work? In lesson one you will lay the foundation for your study of Hebrews by asking yourself, "Why did the author (and God) write the book? What did they want to accomplish? What is the book about?"

In lessons two through eighteen you will analyze successive passages of Hebrews in detail. Thinking about how a paragraph fits into the overall goal of the book will help you to see its purpose. Its purpose will help you see its meaning. Frequently reviewing a chart or outline of the book will enable you to make these connections.

In lesson nineteen you will review Hebrews, returning to the big picture to see whether your view of it has changed after closer study. Review will also strengthen your grasp of major issues and give you an idea of how you have grown from your study.

Kinds of Questions

Bible study on your own—without a structured guide—follows a progression. First you observe: What does the passage *say*? Then you interpret: What does the passage *mean*? Lastly you apply: How does this truth *affect* my life?

Some of the "how" and "why" questions will take some creative thinking, even prayer, to answer. Some are opinion questions without clearcut right answers; these will lend themselves to discussions and side studies.

Don't let your study become an exercise of knowledge alone. Treat the passage as God's Word, and stay in dialogue with Him as you study. Pray, "Lord, what do You want me to see here?" "Father, why is this true?" "Lord, how does this apply to my life?"

It is important that you write down your answers. The act of writing clarifies your thinking and helps you to remember.

Study Aids

A list of reference materials, including a few notes of explanation to help you make good use of them, begins on page 181. This guide is designed to include enough background to let you interpret with just your Bible and the guide. Still, if you want more information on a subject or want to study a book on your own, try the references listed.

Scripture Versions

Unless otherwise indicated, the Bible quotations in this guide are from the New International Version of the Bible. Other versions cited are the Revised Standard Version (RSV), the New American Standard Bible (NASB), and the King James Version (KJV).

Use any translation you like for study, preferably more than one. A paraphrase such as The Living Bible is not accurate enough for study, but it can be helpful for comparison or devotional reading.

Memorizing and Meditating

A psalmist wrote, "I have hidden your word in my heart that I might not sin against you" (Psalm 119:11). If you write down a verse or passage that challenges or encourages you, and reflect on it often for a week or more, you will find it beginning to affect your motives and actions. We forget quickly what we read once; we remember what we ponder.

When you find a significant verse or passage, you might copy it onto a card to keep with you. Set aside five minutes during each day just to think about what the passage might mean in your life. Recite it over to yourself, exploring its meaning. Then, return to your passage as often as you can during your day, for a brief review. You will soon find it coming to mind spontaneously.

For Group Study

A group of four to ten people allows the richest discussions, but you can adapt this guide for other sized groups. It will suit a wide range of group types, such as home Bible studies, growth groups, youth groups, and businessmen's studies. Both new and experienced Bible students, and new and mature Christians, will benefit from the guide. You can omit or leave for later years any questions you find too easy or too hard.

The guide is intended to lead a group through one lesson per week. However, feel free to split lessons if you want to discuss them more thoroughly. Or, omit some questions in a lesson if preparation or discussion time is limited. You can always return to this guide for personal study later. You will be able to discuss only a few questions at length, so choose some for discussion and others for background. Make time at each discussion for members to ask about anything they didn't understand.

Each lesson in the guide ends with a section called "For the group." These sections give advice on how to focus a discussion, how you might apply the lesson in your group, how you might shorten a lesson, and so on. The group leader should read each "For the group" section at least a week ahead so that he or she can tell the group how to prepare for the next lesson.

Each member should prepare for a meeting by writing answers for all of the background and discussion questions to be covered. If the group decides not to take an hour per week for private preparation, then expect to take at least two meetings per lesson to work through the questions. Application will be very difficult, however, without private thought and prayer.

Two reasons for studying in a group are accountability and support. When each member commits in front of the rest to seek growth in an area of life, you can pray with one another, listen jointly for God's guidance, help one another to resist temptation, assure each other that the other's growth matters to you, use the group to practice spiritual principles, and so on. Pray about one another's commitments and needs at most meetings. Spend the first few minutes of each meeting sharing any results from applications prompted by previous lessons. Then discuss new applications toward the end of the meeting. Follow such sharing with prayer for these and other needs.

If you write down each other's applications and prayer requests, you are more likely to remember to pray for them during the week, ask about them at the next meeting, and notice answered prayers. You might want to get a notebook for prayer requests and discussion notes.

Notes taken during discussion will help you to remember, follow up on ideas, stay on the subject, and clarify a total view of an issue. But don't let note-taking keep you from participating. Some groups choose one member at each meeting to take notes. Then someone copies the notes and distributes them at the next meeting. Rotating these tasks can help include more people. Some groups have someone take notes on a large pad of paper or erasable marker board (preformed shower wallboard works well), so that everyone can see what has been recorded.

Pages 184 lists some good sources of counsel for leading group studies.

OVERVIEW

The Book of Hebrews

"To read it is to breathe the atmosphere of heaven itself. To study it is to partake of strong spiritual meat. To abide in its teachings is to be led from immaturity to maturity in the knowledge of Christian truth and of Christ Himself. It is to 'go on unto perfection.'"[1]

The Epistle to the Hebrews reigns unchallenged as the best New Testament commentary on the Old Testament and its relationship to Jesus Christ. It makes clear that the sacrifices and other priestly activities were but shadows pointing forward to Christ, the once-for-all sacrifice for sin, the true Priest, the one mediator between God and man. Indeed, Hebrews may be considered a grand portrait of Christ with the Old Testament as its background.

First impressions

If you are like most people, when you receive an important letter you probably read it straight through first to see what the writer has to say in general. After that, you may go back to examine particular sections more closely. This is just the way to study a biblical letter. In this lesson, you'll take a broad look at Hebrews to lay the groundwork for detailed study in future lessons.

Start by reading the letter through from beginning to end in one sitting. Try reading parts of it aloud, such as 12:1-3,18-29. Get a general impression of what the author is getting at. Think about questions 1 and 2 as you read.

1. Repetition is a clue to the ideas and concepts a writer considers most important to his message. What words and concepts occur over and over in this letter?

   God speaks to his creation.
   The concept of being annointed & — appointed.

_____

_____

_____

2. What seems to be the author's attitude toward his readers? How does he feel about them? (Angry? Thrilled? Frustrated? Impersonal? Compassionate?)

Fatherly type of his concern
Reminding people, reinforcing
what they have already learned.
A position to understand
He is forgiving

3. How does he refer to this letter in 13:22?

exhortation - appeal

4. What do your answers to questions 1 through 3 imply about the author's reasons or aims in writing this letter?

Exalt Jesus as superior to everything

_____

_____

_____

Contrasts

Study Skill—Patterns and Outlines

The first step in an overview is to get some first impressions of the book. Repeated words, the overall mood or tone, the author's attitude toward his readers and his topic—these are all helpful first impressions.

After that, make a broad tentative outline of the book. Start by giving a title to each chapter or main section, and look for patterns that run from section to section. Questions 5 and 8 below point out two such patterns in Hebrews.

5. Briefly scan through the letter once again, this time paying attention to the contrasts the author uses in supporting his main theme.

(1:1-4) Revelation through prophets contrasted with *God speaking to the us through the Son.*

(1:5-2:18) Angels contrasted with *the Son*

(3:1-6) Moses contrasted with _____

(3:12-4:10) Canaan rest contrasted with _____

(4:14-5:10) Aaron's priesthood contrasted with _____

_____

(5:11-14) Spiritual infancy contrasted with _____

Spiritual maturity

maturity in christ

(6:1-20) Apostasy contrasted with *holding onto faith*

(7:1-28) Aaron's priesthood contrasted with *Melchizedek*

(8:1-13) The old covenant contrasted with _____

(9:11-28) Sacrificial blood of animals contrasted with _____

_____

(10:1-18) Repeated Levitical sacrifices contrasted with _____

_____

(10:19-39) Perseverance contrasted with _____

(11:1-40) Faith contrasted with *unbelief*

6. What do these contrasts suggest to you about the author's goal in this letter?

_____

_____

_____

_____

7. In ancient manuscripts, this letter is entitled, *Pros Hebraious*, "To Hebrews." This probably refers to a group of Hebrew Christians. Why do you think the approach you observed in questions 5 and 6 would have been effective with first-century Jewish Christians?

_____

_____

_____

_____

Doctrinal and practical

8. Throughout Hebrews, the author gives theological teaching and then
   says, "Therefore. . . ." Below, summarize the theological points he
   makes in each doctrinal section, then summarize the practical "therefore" that should result from the doctrine.

doctrine (1:1-14) _____

_____

   therefore (2:1) _____

_____

doctrine (2:5-18) _____

_____

   therefore (3:1) _____

_____

doctrine (3:7-19) _____

_____

   therefore (4:1) _____

_____

doctrine (4:6-10) _____

_____

   therefore (4:11) _____

_____

doctrine (5:11-14) _____

_____

   therefore (6:1) _____

_____

doctrine (7:1-10:18) _____

therefore (10:19-22) _____

doctrine (11:1-40) _____

therefore (12:1) _____

doctrine (12:7-11) _____

therefore (12:12) _____

doctrine (12:14-27) _____

therefore (12:28) _____

doctrine (13:11-14) _____

therefore (13:15) _____

Theme and purpose

Study Skill—Themes and Purposes
The point of taking an overview of a book is to start your study with some idea of the message of the book as a whole. Repeated words, the author's mood and feelings about his readers, his own statements about his purposes, and outlines are all clues to the overall message.

You can approach the overall message in two ways. One is to
(continued on page 14)

13

(continued from page 13)
draw out the book's *themes*—main ideas and topics that run through the book. The other is to ask yourself what the author's *purpose* was for writing this letter. Your reasons for studying it might be different than the author's original aims, but you will find it enormously helpful to think about what the Holy Spirit was trying to accomplish with this specific book for its specific first readers. Was He teaching doctrine? Refuting error? Motivating to some particular action? Rebuking some particular sin? Thinking about the author's original purpose will help you get out of a book what the Holy Spirit intends you to get out of it.

When we talk about the author's purpose, we often speak for convenience of the human author. We take for granted that his purpose is in harmony with the Holy Spirit's. If you prefer, you can think of the Holy Spirit instead of the human author. The important thing at this stage is to focus on the letter's purpose for its *original readers.* Later on, this will be a clue to how God wants us to apply the book to ourselves.

9. Based on what you have learned so far, what do you think the author of Hebrews was trying to accomplish with his readers?

10. How would you summarize the main theme(s) of this letter in a sentence?

Study Skill—Background
Once you've made some tentative observations about the themes and aims of a book, you will probably find it helpful to see what others who have studied it extensively think. Commentaries and Bible handbooks (see pages 181-183) offer this information and other helpful background. Below is a summary of such introductory material.

Who wrote it?

As valuable as Hebrews is, little is known with certainty about its occasion, background, and author. Many authors have been suggested through the centuries; the three most worthy of mention are Paul, Apollos, and Barnabas. Paul is well-known as the founder of a dozen key churches and the writer of thirteen other New Testament letters. Apollos was a Jew from Egypt, who became a great Christian teacher and whom Paul mentioned as an equal (Acts 18:24-28; 1 Corinthians 3:5-6; 4:1,6). Barnabas, another Jewish Christian leader, was Paul's senior partner in ministry until Paul grew into a mature apostle (Acts 4:36-37, 11:25-26, 13:1-3, 15:36-41; 1 Corinthians 9:6). Any of these men had the stature to pen a letter with the Holy Spirit's stamp of authority.

All we know for certain about the author is that he was thoroughly familiar with the Jewish religious system, that he and his readers knew each other (6:9; 13:18,19,23-24), and that Paul's aide Timothy was known to both (13:23). Whoever he was, the author was a superb writer as well as an inspired thinker; his Greek is the most elegant in the New Testament. "We may compare it [Hebrews] to a painting of perfect beauty, which has been regarded as a work of Raphael. If it should be proved that it was not painted by Raphael, we have thereby not lost a classical piece of art, but gained another master of first rank."[2]

Who received it?

Whatever is known today of the original readers is derived from the epistle itself. The earliest manuscripts have the simple title "To Hebrews." This group was apparently a single congregation of Hebrew Christians living somewhere in the Roman world (5:11-12, 6:9-10, 13:23-24). Precisely where? Suggestions include Jerusalem, Alexandria, Caesarea, Ephesus, Rome, and Syrian Antioch, but no one knows for certain.

In the final analysis, the precise destination is no more important than the author's identity. "Regardless of who wrote it, or where it was first sent, the Christian church has rightly regarded it down through the ages as a powerfully relevant message from God, who has definitively spoken in His Son."[3]

The situation

The writer makes it clear that this group of Jewish believers was going through severe persecution (10:32-34), probably on religious grounds, by nonChristian Jews.

For a first-century Jew to become a believer in Jesus Christ required a great sacrifice. He was immediately branded as an apostate and a blemish to the Jewish nation. He was considered "unclean" in the strongest possible sense. Defecting Jews were immediately expelled from the synagogue; their children were denied the privilege of attending the synagogue school; they lost their jobs in geographical areas controlled by the Jews; in short, they lost everything of earthly value to them. Furthermore, the Jewish high priest had the authority in Judea, and to some extent in other provinces, to throw troublesome Jews in jail (compare 10:33-34). It was circumstances such as these that apparently caused many of these Hebrew believers to wane in their commitment to Christ.

At first, these Hebrew Christians joyfully accepted persecution (10:34). But after a while, it apparently became too much for them to bear and their endurance weakened (10:35-36). The warning passages in the letter suggest that these believers were degenerating in faith. While they never considered actually renouncing Jesus Christ, they nevertheless contemplated drifting back into the outward observances of Judaism (including rituals, ceremonies, and sacrifices—see 2:1, 4:14, 7:11, 10:1, 13:9-14). They apparently reasoned that if they took part in such rites, the Jewish leaders might be satisfied and leave them alone.

The writer set out to warn them about the futility of such reasoning. If they lapsed from Christianity back into Judaism—as they had already begun to do to some extent—they would be identifying themselves with an obsolete system and a Christ-rejecting nation that was under judgment. The writer accordingly pointed them to a better way. His argument was revolutionary: Because of Christ, everything is new. Everything is better. The old has passed away, so hold onto your faith and commitment. Don't retrogress. Instead, patiently endure your present circumstances. Your faith will be generously rewarded. This is certain, for God's promise cannot fail.

Your response

11. What are some of the questions that you would like to have answered as you delve more deeply into Hebrews? (Your questions can serve as personal objectives for your study.)

_____

_____

_____

_____

_____

_____

_____

_____

12. Did your overview of Hebrews suggest any areas of your life that you want to work on during this study? If so, jot them down, along with any plans you already have to deal with them. Take each one to God in prayer, asking Him to show you His priorities for your application and to give you His strength to become what He desires. If anything in the book has convicted you, confess your failings to God.

_____

_____

_____

_____

_____

For the group

This "For the group" section and the ones in later lessons suggest ways of structuring your discussions. Feel free to select what suits your group and ignore the rest. The main goals of this lesson are to get to know Hebrews as a whole and the people with whom you are going to study it.

Worship. Some groups like to begin with prayer and/or singing. Some share requests for prayer at the beginning, but leave the actual prayer until after the study. Others prefer just to chat for awhile and then move to the study, leaving worship until the end. It is a good idea to start with at least a brief prayer for the Holy Spirit's guidance and some silence to help everyone change focus from the day's busyness to the Scripture.

Warm-up. The beginning of a new study is a good time to lay a foundation for honest sharing of ideas, to get comfortable with each other, and to encourage a sense of common purpose. One way to establish common ground is to talk about what each group member hopes to get out of your group—out of your study of Hebrews, and out of any prayer, singing, sharing, outreach, or anything else you might do together. Why do you want to study the Bible, and Hebrews in particular? If you have someone write down each member's hopes and expectations, then you can look back at these goals later to see if they are being met. Allow about fifteen minutes for this discussion so that it does not degenerate into vague chatting.

How to use this study. If the group has never used a LIFECHANGE study guide before, you might take a whole meeting to get acquainted, discuss your goals, and go over the "How to Use This Study" section on pages 5-8. Then you can take a second meeting to discuss the overview. This will assure that everyone understands the study and will give you more time to read all of Hebrews and answer the overview questions.

Go over the parts of the "How to Use This Study" section that you think the group should especially notice. For example, point out the optional questions in the margins. These are available as questions for group discussion, ideas for application, and suggestions for further study. It is unlikely that anyone will have the time or desire to answer all the optional questions. A person might do one "Optional Application" for any given lesson. You might choose one or two "For Thought and Discussions" for your group discussion, or you might spend all your time on the numbered questions. If someone wants to write answers to the optional questions, suggest that he use a separate notebook. It will also be helpful for discussion notes, prayer requests, answers to prayers, application plans, and so on.

Invite everyone to ask questions about how to use the study guide and how your discussions will go.

Reading. It is often helpful to refresh everyone's memory by reading the passage aloud before discussing the questions. Reading all of Hebrews is probably unreasonable, so choose a couple of passages that evoke the book's flavor, such as 1:1-4 and 12:18-29. Try to make the letter sound like a living person talking.

First impressions. Ask group members to share their answers to questions 1, 2, and 3. Questions 4, 6, and 7 probably don't need discussing. To avoid making question 5 tedious, go around the room taking turns stating each contrast. Likewise for question 8, go around the room taking turns stating a doctrine and its "therefore." Then invite answers to questions 9 and 10.

Questions. Give everyone a chance to share questions about the historical background (in this lesson) and the letter. It is good to clear up any confusion as early as possible. However, don't answer any questions that deal with specific passages. Write those down and let the group answer them when you get to the passages.

Some people dislike giving any attention to the human author of inspired Scripture because this seems to denigrate its divine authority. If necessary, explain that this series takes the view that just as Jesus was fully God and fully Man, so the books of the Bible are eternal messages from the Spirit of God and messages from particular men in particular times and places. Just as Jesus' humanity and divinity are both essential to His mission and nature, so the humanity and divinity of the biblical books are both important. When we refer to the human writer of this letter, we are in no way denying divine inspiration.

Application. If application is new to some group members, you might make up some sample applications together. Choose a paragraph or verse and think of how it is relevant to you and some specific things you could each do about it. Share your answers to question 12.

Wrap-up. The group leader should have read lesson two and its "For the group" section. At this point, he or she might give a short summary of what members can expect in that lesson and the coming meeting. This is a chance to whet everyone's appetite, assign any optional questions, omit any numbered questions, or forewarn members of possible difficulties.

Encourage any members who found the overview especially difficult. Some people are better at seeing the big picture than others. Some are best at analyzing a particular verse or paragraph, while others are strongest at seeing how a passage applies to their lives. Urge members to give thanks for their own and others' strengths, and to give and request help when needed. The group is a place to learn from each other. Later lessons will draw on the gifts of close analyzers as well as overviewers and appliers, practical as well as theoretical thinkers.

Worship. Many groups like to end with singing and/or prayer. This can include songs and prayers that respond to what you've learned in Hebrews or prayers for specific needs of group members. Some people are shy about sharing personal needs or praying aloud in groups, especially before they know the other people well. If this is true of your group, then a song and/or some silent prayer, and a short closing prayer spoken by the leader, might be an appropriate end. You could also share requests and pray in pairs.

1. E. Schuyler English, *Studies in the Epistle to the Hebrews* (Neptune, New Jersey: Louzeaux Brothers, 1976), page 11.
2. Thiersch, cited by English, page 26.
3. Zane C. Hodges, "Hebrews," *The Bible Knowledge Commentary* (Wheaton: Victor Books, 1983), page 780.

Outline of Hebrews

You can find a variety of helpful outlines of Hebrews in commentaries and Bible handbooks. Here is one possibility.

Theme: Since Christ is supreme, God's people must look only to Him.

I. THE SUPERIORITY OF CHRIST
   Christ is superior to all Old Testament characters and institutions.
   A. (1:1-4) Christ is superior to the prophets.
   B. (1:5-2:18) Christ is superior to the angels.
   C. (3:1-6) Christ is superior to Moses.
   D. (3:7-19) Therefore, avoid unbelief.
   E. (4:1-16) The consequences and cure for unbelief.
   F. (5:1-10) Christ has superior priestly qualifications.
   G. (5:11-6:12) Warning: don't fall away.
   H. (6:13-20) God is worthy of trust, for His promise is certain.
   I. (7:1-28) Christ's priestly order is superior to Aaron's.
   J. (8:1-13) Christ is the priest of a new and superior covenant.
   K. (9:1-10:18) Christ's sanctuary and sacrifice are superior.

II. PERSEVERING IN FAITH
   Patiently endure.
   A. (10:19-39) Persevere.
   B. (11:1-40) Maintain faith in Christ.
   C. (12:1-29) Accept God's discipline and remain committed to Him.
   D. (13:1-21) Exercise love.
   E. (13:22-25) Closing remarks.

HEBREWS 1:1-4

Christ Superior to Prophets

This group of Hebrew Christians is under severe pressure to turn back to Judaism. Fierce persecution from orthodox Jewish leaders is undermining their commitment to Jesus Christ. The writer accordingly exhorts them repeatedly to *endure patiently.*

Imagine yourself in the situation of the persecuted Jewish Christians. How would this opening paragraph help you respond to persecution with patient endurance?

Read 1:1-4 once silently and once aloud to yourself. Ask God to speak to you through these verses.

At many times (1:1). NASB: "in many portions." Revelation in the Old Testament was fragmentary and was given on many different occasions. Each such revelation contained only a portion of the truth. Therefore, we speak of "progressive revelation" in the Old Testament.

Study Skill—Cross-references
Other parts of Scripture often shed light on a passage you are studying. These are called "cross-references." A concordance (see page 182) or a study Bible can help you find your own cross-references.

(handwritten margin note, top left) God will not leave until his promise is fulfilled

1. Examine the following passages and list some of the "various ways" that God spoke to men in days past.

   Genesis 28:10-15 _Jacob: through dreams & visions_

   Exodus 3:1-6 (especially verse 2) _burning bush_

   Exodus 20:1-21 _in person – 10 commandments_

   Exodus 31:18 _tablets of stone_

   2 Peter 1:21 _as men were moved by the Holy Spirit._

Last days (1:2). The last days began when God spoke finally and completely in the incarnation, crucifixion, and resurrection of His Son.

Heir of all things (1:2). As the Son of God, Christ owns all things in the universe. Consequently, He is rightfully the Controller, Sovereign, and Lord of all things.

(handwritten margin note, bottom left) Historically documented fact / bore out in the / bore already / things told

2. What do you see in 1:1-2 that indicates a basic unity between the Old and New Testaments?

   God is speaking revelation of Himself.

22

3. There are three contrasts between 1:1 and 1:2. List them.

1:1	1:2

4. How do these contrasts contribute to the author's purpose in writing this letter? (Recall your answer to question 9 on page 14.)

_____

_____

_____

_____

_____

_____

5. The concept that Jesus is God's ultimate revelation is weighty. How has God spoken to us by His Son (Hebrews 1:2)? (*Optional:* Read John 1:14, 12:44-46, 14:9-11.)

The Lord walked the earth —
word became flesh.

_____

_____

_____

For Further Study:
a. For more on Jesus as the "heir of all things," see Psalm 2:8; Matthew 28:18; John 3:35; 10:29; 16:15; 17:2,6.
b. Those who trust in Christ are called co-heirs with Him (Romans 8:17, Galatians 4:7). What are the implications of this for your life and actions?

For Further Study:
a. What method did God use to bring the universe into being (Genesis 1:1-26, Hebrews 11:3)?
b. How does this relate to Christ sustaining the universe "by his powerful word"?

6. What difference does it make to you that Jesus is "heir of all things" and that the Father made the universe through Him (Hebrews 1:2)?

Nothing belongs to anyone but Christ

Radiance (1:3). Literally, "shining forth." The word indicates not a reflection but an outshining of resplendent light. Jesus Christ shines forth to the world the very character, attributes, and essence of God (John 1:14).

Exact representation (1:3). In classical Greek, this phrase was used of an engraving tool or stamp, often in minting coins. In common usage, it came to refer to the actual mark engraved or the impression made by the tool itself. Thus, the word implies an exact expression. Jesus is the absolutely authentic representation of God's being (John 14:9).

Sustaining all things (1:3). Not just upholding all things in the sense of Atlas holding the dead weight of a world. "Sustaining" includes the idea of movement toward a determined end. Jesus maintains and carries along all things in the universe (Colossians 1:17).

Right hand (1:3). In Jewish culture, sitting at the right hand was a place of honor, privilege, dignity, and power. That Christ *sat down* at this exalted place indicates that His work was finished.

7. There are five "proofs" in Hebrews 1:3 that Christ is fully God. List these in your own words.

a. _brightness of His glory_

b. _perfect copy of God - expressed image_

c. _empowered_

d. _purged - atonement_

e. _at His right hand_

8. Why do you think the author makes such a point of Christ's deity to these Hebrew Christians?

_____

_____

_____

_____

_____

9. What difference does it make to you that Jesus sustains everything by His powerful Word (1:3)?

He holds us together by the power of His word

_____

_____

For Further Study:
a. For more on how Jesus accomplishes mighty things by His "powerful word," see Matthew 8:8-13; Mark 1:40-42, 4:35-41; Luke 7:14-15; John 11:38-43.
b. Also on God's creative Word, see Psalms 33:6-9, 148:1-5.

For Thought and Discussion: Explain what Jesus accomplished while on earth (Hebrews 1:3, 7:27).

For Further Study: For more on how Jesus' blood redeems us, see Exodus 12:1-4,13; Leviticus 16:1-34; Deuteronomy 21:1-9; Romans 3:21-26.

Angels (1:4). The Jews considered angels to be extremely powerful and highly exalted beings. They were especially revered because they were

For Thought and Discussion: a. What in 1:2 indicates Christ's relationship to the angels?
b. What does this say about His revelation versus theirs?

For Further Study: On angels as created beings, see Psalm 148:2-5, John 1:3, Colossians 1:16.

Optional Application: Reflect on the fact that the entire universe was created through Jesus Christ. (See Psalm 95, for example.) How should a creature respond to its Creator? How can you put this into practice this week?

Optional Application: Is anything in your life tempting you to lapse in your commitment to Christ? If so, what in 1:1-4 might help you endure patiently? Meditate on this truth this week.

the intermediaries by whom God gave the Law to Moses on Mount Sinai (2 Samuel 14:20, Psalm 103:20, Hebrews 12:22).

Name (1:4). According to ancient Jewish thinking, a name represented a person's full character in all that he was and did. Names were a mini-commentary on the person.

Two names that Jesus has received are "Christ" and "Lord" (Acts 2:36, Philippians 2:9-11). In Jewish circles, "Christ" meant the man anointed to be king of Israel, and "Lord" was the usual way of referring to God.

10. What other name did Jesus receive (Hebrews 1:5)?

Son

11. Angels took part in communicating God's revelation in the Old Testament. What does 1:4 imply about the revelation given through Christ as compared to that given through angels?

Superiority

12. How would you summarize the author's main point in 1:1-4?

Jesus as son expresses all there is about the godhead. He is all he claims to be

Your response

13. What one insight from 1:1-4 seems most personally significant to you right now?

Joint heir

26

_____

_____

_____

14. How would you like this truth to affect your life—your thoughts, attitudes, habits, and priorities?

established confidence

_____

_____

_____

_____

15. What action can you take this week to start putting this into practice or to cooperate with God in bringing about this transformation?

learn the word

_____

_____

_____

_____

16. If you have any questions about 1:1-4, write them down so that you can remember to seek answers.

_____

_____

_____

_____

For the group

Warm-up. People often come to Bible studies with their minds still churning over the day's events. Singing and prayer can help people refocus onto

God and His Word. Another method you may find helpful is to begin with a question that deals with people's lives and is related to the topic at hand. For this lesson, you might open by going around the room and letting each person respond to this question: "How has God spoken to you this week?" You don't want to have a discussion about a warm-up question. Its purpose is simply to draw the group together and give you some idea of where everyone is mentally and spiritually.

Read aloud. Ask someone to read 1:1-4 aloud.

Summarize. Glance at the forest before focusing on the trees by having someone state his or her answer to question 12.

Questions. The doctrine that Christ is fully God is as much under fire today as in the first century. Some say He was just a moral teacher, while others regard Him as a human being who made His body available to the cosmic Christ spirit for three short years. Others believe generally in His divinity, but are vague about the implications of this. So, discuss what 1:1-4 implies about Christ's identity. Then, examine how these facts should affect your attitudes toward yourself, your security, your world.

Don't worry if you can't get through all of the questions (number 1, for example), as long as you wrestle with some aspects of the passage deeply enough to come to some conclusions about how it applies to you. Encourage each group member to come up with one implication to focus on during the coming week, and one specific step he or she can take to make this truth a part of his or her life.

Summarize. It's a good idea to return to the big picture at the end of your discussion. Ask one or two people to summarize briefly what 1:1-4 is about and how it is relevant to your lives.

Prayer. Thank God for speaking to you through His Son. Praise Jesus for all that you have learned about Him—for being the radiance of God's glory, for providing purification for sins, and so on. Ask Him to help you trust Him to sustain all things by His Word and to purify each of you from sin.

28

HEBREWS 1:5-2:18

Christ Superior to Angels

Most people don't think about angels very much today. But to a first-century Jew, angels were the greatest beings in the universe under God. And there are still groups today who think Christ was only a high angel or spirit being. To see how the writer to the Hebrews responds to these notions, review 1:1-4 and read 1:5-2:18 aloud to yourself.

> ### Study Skill—Reading Aloud
> When you read silently to yourself, you take in information just through your eyes, but when you read aloud, you hear it as well as see it. You also have to slow down and notice each word as you pronounce it. For both of these reasons, most people find they get much more of a grasp of a passage when they read it aloud than when they read it silently.

The Son is superior (1:5-14)

Firstborn (1:6). This title basically means "chief one." "He is called 'the firstborn' because He exists before all creation and because all creation is His heritage."[1]

Winds . . . fire (1:7). Some scholars believe the author is suggesting that angels often blend their mutable natures with winds or fire as they

For Thought and Discussion: a. From where does the author obtain the bulk of his information to support his points in this passage (1:5-13; 2:6-8,12-13)?

b. Why was this an effective approach for his particular readers?

For Thought and Discussion: Hebrews 1:4 says that Christ inherited a superior name to that of the angels. What is that name (1:5), and how is it significant to the argument in 1:5-18?

For Further Study: For more on the Sonship of Christ, see Psalm 2:7-12, Matthew 3:17, Luke 1:32, Acts 13:32-33, Romans 1:4.

perform the tasks God gives them (Psalm 104:4). Others believe the author is portraying angels as executing God's commands with the swiftness of wind and the strength of fire.

Right hand (1:13). A place of honor, dignity, power, and authority.

1. In 1:5-14, the author uses seven familiar Old Testament passages to draw explicit contrasts between Christ and the angels. List these contrasts.

	Christ	angels
1:5		
1:6		
1:7-9		

	Christ	angels
1:10-12		
1:13-14		

For Further Study:
Read Genesis 1:1, a passage inscribed on the Jewish mind from childhood. In light of this verse, how do you think Hebrews 1:10 would have affected Jewish readers, and why?

For Further Study:
On how the heavens and the earth will perish (Hebrews 1:11), see 2 Peter 3:10-13.

2. What do you think the cumulative effect of these contrasts would have been on a Jewish Christian who was contemplating lapsing back into the externals of Judaism? Why?

_____

_____

_____

_____

_____

3. Scripture declares that God alone is the proper object of worship (Exodus 34:14, Revelation 19:9-10). First-century Jews knew this well. What implications does this have for your understanding of Hebrews 1:6?

_____

_____

For Further Study:
The author of
Hebrews quotes or
alludes to Psalm 110
repeatedly (1:13;
5:6,10; 6:20;
7:3,11,21; 8:1;
10:12-13; 12:2).
Study the whole of
this psalm to see the
cited passages in
context.

**Optional
Application:** The
author refers to
angels as "minister-
ing spirits" (1:14).
Have you ever been
aware of their minis-
try to you? Meditate
for a few moments on
Psalm 91:9-12, and
consider the practical
implications this pas-
sage has for your life.
How should you
respond?

**For Thought and
Discussion:** Who
gives each of the
names in question 4a
to Christ, and why is
this important
(1:6,8,10,13)?

4. One of the ways the author demonstrates
Christ's superiority in chapter 1 is by sprinkling
proofs of His deity throughout.

a. What divine names and descriptions are
ascribed to Christ (1:5,8,10)?

_____

_____

_____

_____

_____

_____

b. What works did Christ do that only God could
do (1:2-3,10)?

_____

_____

_____

_____

c. How else is He portrayed as divine
(1:3,10-13)?

_____

_____

_____

_____

32

Pay attention (2:1-4)

For Thought and Discussion: How is "what we have heard" (2:1) related to 1:2?

For Thought and Discussion: a. How do you or other modern Christians tend to "drift away" from God, or fail to "pay . . . careful attention" to what He has said (2:1)?
b. What restorative steps would you advise for those who have drifted away from God or failed to pay attention to His Word?

For if (2:2). "Argument in the rabbinic style, from the lesser to the greater; from the giving of the Law by angels to the greater giving of the Gospel by Christ."[2]

Message spoken by angels (2:2). The Law given to Moses at Mount Sinai (Deuteronomy 33:2; Psalm 68:17; Acts 7:38,53; Galatians 3:19).

Just punishment (2:2). This punishment was often drastic. Two of Aaron's sons were consumed by fire from the altar for offering "unauthorized fire before the LORD, contrary to his command" (Leviticus 10:1). A group of several hundred Israelites was swallowed up in a sudden crack in the earth or consumed by fire for rebelling against Moses' leadership (Numbers 16:1-35).

For Thought and Discussion: How is each Person of the Trinity involved in the delivery and confirmation of the salvation message (2:3-4)? (Keep in mind that in the New Testament, "Lord" usually refers to Christ and "God" normally refers to the Father.)

For Thought and Discussion: Hebrews 2:1-4 illustrates the principle that the more light one receives, the more severe the punishment for violating or ignoring that light. Read Matthew 11:20-24 and Luke 12:47-48, and examine how these passages relate to and support this principle. What implications does this principle have for your life?

Plagues regularly ravaged Israel's camp when the people rebelled (Exodus 32:35, Numbers 16:41-50). Deuteronomy 28:15-68 details the calamities that would befall Israel if the nation broke the covenant.

Study Skill—Rhetorical Questions
A rhetorical question is one "to which no answer is expected, or to which only one answer may be made."[3] Think about this: Is the question in Hebrews 2:2-3 rhetorical? Why or why not?

5. According to 2:3-4, the message of salvation came to this group of believers with a threefold authority and validation. Explain each in your own words.

"first announced by . . ." (2:3) _____

_____

_____

_____

"confirmed to us by . . ." (2:3) _____

_____

_____

(2:4) _____

_____

_____

6. In light of all of 1:5-2:4, summarize why these Hebrew Christians were in greater danger if they ignored "such a great salvation" than the danger of those who violated the Old Testament Law.

_____

_____

_____

34

For Further Study:
For more on how God added His confirmation to the gospel message with "signs, wonders, and various miracles," look at Acts 2:43; 3:1-16; 4:29-31; 5:12-16; 6:8; 8:4-7; 14:3,8-20; 2 Corinthians 12:12.

7. How can a person ignore the great salvation while still saying and thinking that he or she believes in Christ?

_____

_____

_____

_____

_____

For Further Study:
a. The context of Psalm 8 points back to the creation account in Genesis. Read Genesis 1:26-27 and summarize what you learn about man's intended role on earth.
   b. What happened to the glory, honor, and dominion originally given to man? (See Genesis 3:1-24.)

Jesus made like His brothers (2:5-18)

Under his feet (2:8). In ancient times, the king's throne was elevated so that everyone who visited him had to bow down before him, sometimes even kissing his feet. His subjects were accordingly said to be "under his feet." The feet were considered the lowliest part of the body, so to be under someone's feet was to have lower status than him.

8. Read Psalm 8:3-8. In this psalm, David expresses astonishment at God's concern for puny man. What does Psalm 8:6-8 say about man's God-appointed role on earth?

_____

_____

_____

_____

_____

_____

35

For Thought and Discussion: In what ways is man "a little lower than the angels" (2:7)?

For Thought and Discussion: What is God's ultimate goal for humans (2:10a)?

In Hebrews 2:5-9, the author applies Psalm 8:4-6 to Jesus as a perfect representative man, in whom man's restoration to glory and his appointed destiny to rule will ultimately be fully realized. Jesus is the forerunner of what all believers will become.

9. Sin marred man's intended glory. Instead of being God's vice-regent on earth, man became enslaved to sin, fear of death, and Satan (Hebrews 2:15). What did Christ do to make it possible for all men to be restored to glory and honor (2:9)?

_____

_____

_____

_____

_____

It was fitting (2:10). Consistent with God's divine character and wisdom.

Author (2:10). Leader, originator, founder. The Greeks commonly used this word for a "pioneer who blazed a trail for others to follow."[4] Jesus, as the "author of . . . salvation," is a pioneer of salvation for His brothers to follow.

Holy (2:11). This primarily means set apart for God. It also implies moral purity.

10. How does the author stress Jesus' complete identity with man in 2:11-13?

_____

_____

_____

_____

_____

Destroy (2:14). Annul, bring to naught, make of no effect. (NASB: "render powerless.")

11. Why did Jesus have to share human nature completely (2:14-18)?

_____

_____

_____

_____

_____

12. What three purposes for Christ's death do you see in 2:14-17?

2:14 _____

_____

2:15 _____

_____

2:17 _____

_____

High priest (2:17). The author will develop Jesus' role as priest at length in chapters 5 through 10. Basically, a priest represents man before God in religious rites so that man and God may be brought together in relationship.

Make atonement for (2:17). NASB: "make propitiation for." The penalty for sin (rebellion against God) is death (Romans 6:23). But God does not want sinners to die. The Old Testament sacrificial system was designed to illuminate both God's just hatred of sin and His merciful desire not to punish. God allowed men to kill animals in place of themselves. These sacrifices "atoned for" (covered or made satisfaction for) sin, "expiated" (removed) man's guilt, and "propi-

Optional Application: Do you ever feel enslaved by the fear of death (2:15)? If so, what have you learned in this lesson that helps you come to grips with and let go of this fear? Take time daily this week to meditate on this truth, letting it sink deep into your heart.

For Thought and Discussion: a. One of the duties of a high priest is to represent human beings before God. How do the temptations of Christ help Him in His high priestly duties (2:18)?
  b. Why is it important that no trial or temptation can come upon believers that Christ does not perfectly understand?

Optional Application: a. Scan through 1:5-2:18, trying to imagine the impact these verses would have had on Jewish Christians in the first century. Which statements or arguments do you think would have most firmly convinced you to remain committed to Christ and not lapse back into religious externals?
b. How are these statements relevant to your current life?

Optional Application: The author refers to what Christ accomplished in His death as "such a great salvation" (2:3). Make a list of some reasons why you personally consider God's salvation to be so great. Then, give praise to God for what He has accomplished for you.

tiated" (satisfied, appeased) God's justice. See Leviticus 16:11,15-16,20-22.

Those Old Testament sacrifices were not sufficient payment for sin in themselves; they were sufficient only in that they represented what Christ was going to do. By putting faith in the sacrifices commanded for cleansing sin, the Israelites were putting faith in God's way of cleansing that is fully revealed in Christ.

13. Since Jesus was sinless, suffering did not make Him morally or spiritually perfect. How, then, did suffering make the "author of . . . salvation perfect" (2:10)? (According to 2:18, in what area did suffering make Christ perfect?)

_____

_____

_____

_____

_____

Study Skill—Outlining
Making an outline can help you trace the author's reasoning in a passage. Start by summarizing what the whole passage is about. Then divide it into paragraphs—places where the author's train of thought shifts. Give each paragraph a title. If you like, add subpoints under each paragraph title.
The outline on page 20 gives titles to major passages. Starting from it or from scratch, begin an outline of Hebrews with 1:1-2:18. Make up titles for 1:1-4 and 1:5-2:18, then give titles to each paragraph in 1:5-2:18. The subtitles in this lesson may help you.

Your response

14. What one insight from 1:5-2:18 seems most like something you want to take to heart?

38

_____

_____

_____

_____

_____

15. How would you like this truth to affect your life in concrete ways?

_____

_____

_____

_____

16. What action can you take to cooperate with God in bringing this about?

_____

_____

_____

_____

_____

17. List any questions you have about 1:5–2:18.

_____

_____

_____

_____

Optional Application: a. How does Christ's role as high priest encourage you in your current situation (2:17-18)? Do you think He really understands everything you are going through?
b. Are there any areas of your life that are presently causing you to suffer, and that you would now like to entrust to your high priest who understands and can do something about them?

For the group

Warm-up. Ask everyone to think for a moment about this question: "What aspect of yourself or your circumstances would you say is your biggest obstacle to paying careful attention to (and acting on) what God has said through and about His Son?" (You may have to read this rather long question a couple of times.) Then let anyone answer who wishes to.

Read aloud and summarize.

Questions. The focus in this lesson is on how we know that Christ is fully God and fully human: the contrast between Christ and the angels; how we know that Christ is God; why Christ was made like humans. When you think you have a grasp of these crucial truths, discuss how they are relevant to each of your lives.

Summarize.

Prayer. Praise Jesus for being the eternal Son of God, worthy of worship, participant with the Father in creation, and ruler of the world. Praise Him for lowering Himself to become human in all ways so that He could understand and deal with your sufferings and temptations. Ask Him to help you worship Him as God, depend on Him as high priest, and hold fast to the truth you know.

Angels in Judaism

Angels were the object of much discussion among Jews between 200 BC and 400 AD. Although some of what they believed was rooted in the Old Testament, a great deal of speculation also went into the writings of the rabbis.

First-century Jews believed that angels were the highest beings in creation next to God (who was thought to be surrounded by innumerable angels). The Jews were convinced that such angels were the primary instruments of bringing God's Word to men and of working out His will in the physical universe. Both the Hebrew and Greek words for "angel" simply meant "messenger" and were used as such in secular contexts (a military courier was called an *angelos* in Greek).

Many Jews believed that the angels acted as God's "senate" or "supreme council," and that God did nothing without consulting this council. These Jews interpreted the "us" in "Let us make

(continued on page 41)

(continued from page 40)
man in our image" (Genesis 1:26) as a reference to the deliberations of the angelic council.

According to Jewish thought, God assigned to angels various tasks as operators of the universe. Two hundred angels controlled the movements of the stars. Another mighty angel managed the seas, while others superintended the frost, dew, rain, snow, hail, thunder, and lightning. Still others were the wardens of hell and torturers of the damned. There were even recording angels who—in order to assist God in His future judgment of humanity—wrote down every word men spoke.

It was commonly believed that the Law of Moses was brought from God to Israel by angels. This was the primary reason why the Jews so revered them. They believed that the angels were actually the mediators of their covenant with God, and that the angels were charged with ministering the blessings of the covenant to them.

It was in this context that the writer to the Hebrews set out to prove Christ's superiority over angels.

1. F.F. Bruce, *The Epistle to the Hebrews* (Grand Rapids, Michigan: William B. Eerdmans Publishing Company, 1979), page 15.
2. Robert W. Ross, "Hebrews," *The Wycliffe Bible Commentary,* edited by Charles F. Pfeiffer and Everett F. Harrison (Chicago: Moody Press, 1974), page 1410.
3. *The American Heritage Dictionary of the English Language,* edited by William Morris (Boston: Houghton Mifflin Company, 1978), page 1114.
4. MacArthur, page 66.

HEBREWS 3:1-6

Christ Superior to Moses

In Jewish thinking, almost everything of importance relating to God was somehow connected to Moses. He was the highest example of human faithfulness to God. He was the redeemer and leader of the nation. In fact, the Messiah was expected to be a prophet like Moses (Deuteronomy 18:15). A comparison between Jesus and Moses was obligatory. Read 3:1-6 twice, at least once aloud.

Fix your thoughts (3:1). Thoughtfully and attentively consider. The phrase implies both concentrated attention and continuous observation. "The idea is, 'Put your mind on Jesus and let it remain there, that you may understand who He is and what He wills.'"[1]

1. Notice that 3:1 begins with "Therefore." Briefly summarize the doctrinal truth in 2:5-18 that is the basis for the application in 3:1.

_____

_____

_____

_____

_____

For Thought and Discussion: The phrase "holy brothers who share in the heavenly calling" (3:1) unites three strands of truth found in 2:10-12. What do these verses say about holiness, brotherhood, and sharing in the heavenly calling?

For Further Study: What do Ephesians 2:6-7 and Revelation 7:15-17, 21:1-22:5 say about our heavenly calling?

43

Optional Application: To what kind of life does the fact that you "share in the heavenly calling" (3:1) motivate you? What specific actions can you take along this line?

For Thought and Discussion: Jesus holds both of the foundational offices (apostle and high priest) of the new covenant. What does this tell you about Him?

2. What do you learn about your heavenly calling (3:1) from the following passages?

Philippians 3:20-21 _____

_____

_____

2 Timothy 2:12 _____

_____

Revelation 21:1-4 _____

_____

_____

_____

3. Why do you think the author reminded his Hebrew readers that they were "holy brothers who share in the heavenly calling" (3:1)?

_____

_____

_____

_____

Apostle (3:1). Literally, "one who is sent"—a messenger, proxy, or ambassador. In Jewish law, the *apostolos* (Greek) or *shaliach* (Aramaic) was "a person acting with full authority for another" in a business or legal transaction.[2] Moses was considered God's *shaliach* in establishing the covenant between God and Israel, while his brother Aaron was the high priest who mediated between God and man in the sacrifices. Jesus is both the *shaliach* and the high priest of the new covenant.

As apostle, Jesus pleads God's cause with believers. As high priest, He pleads the believer's cause with God. These two concepts com-

44

bine in the idea that Jesus is our "mediator" (1 Timothy 2:5-6).

4. For what mission was Jesus sent?

John 4:34; 5:24,30,36-38; 6:38 _____

_____

_____

_____

_____

_____

Galatians 4:4-5, 1 John 4:10 _____

_____

For Thought and Discussion: How is Jesus uniquely qualified to be the ultimate high priest, representing man before God (2:17-18)?

Optional Application: What are some of the things that are presently distracting you from fixing your thoughts on Jesus? What can you do about these?

5. Why is it important to "fix your thoughts" on your apostle and high priest?

_____

_____

_____

_____

6. Moses and Jesus are alike in that both were "faithful" to the One who appointed them (Hebrews 3:2). God said Moses was faithful in all His house (Numbers 12:7). How did each man demonstrate faithfulness?

Moses (Exodus 3:10, 40:16) _____

_____

_____

_____

For Further Study:
What do Luke
24:25-26,44 and John
5:46 show about
Jesus' superiority to
Moses?

Jesus (John 17:5, Colossians 1:13-14) _____

_____

_____

_____

_____

7. Why was Jesus' act of faithfulness greater?

_____

_____

_____

_____

_____

8. The Jews esteemed Moses as their greatest
leader (Deuteronomy 34:10-12). How do you
think first-century Jewish Christians would have
reacted to Hebrews 3:3?

_____

_____

_____

_____

9. "God is the builder of everything" (3:4), the
writer comments. What does this say about
Jesus as opposed to Moses (3:3)?

_____

_____

_____

_____

10. How else was Jesus' faithfulness greater than
Moses' (3:5-6)?

_____

_____

_____

_____

_____

Hold on (3:6). Literally, "hold fast and firm to the end." The word was often used in nautical circles with the meaning of "holding one's course toward." In 3:6 it means "stay on course in what God has revealed for your lives and be careful not to veer or drift away."

11. When the author says "we are his house" (3:6), who do you think he is referring to, and what does he mean? (*Optional:* See Ephesians 2:19-22, 1 Peter 2:5.)

_____

_____

_____

_____

12. What do you think is the significance of the "if" clause at the end of Hebrews 3:6?

_____

_____

_____

_____

Hope (3:6). This Greek word does not mean a mood of wishfulness, but rather something one expects with confidence.

For Further Study: Scholars have long debated the meaning of the "if" clause in Hebrews 3:6. What do you learn about this issue from Mark 4:1-3,9,13-20; John 8:31; 2 Corinthians 13:5; Hebrews 3:14; 10:23?

For Thought and Discussion: What do you think "the hope of which we boast" (3:6) is? See what else the author says about hope in 6:11,18-19; 7:18-19; 11:1.

47

For Thought and Discussion: The author has demonstrated Christ's superiority over prophets (1:1-4), angels (1:5-2:8), and Moses (3:1-6). Why was this a wise approach for dealing with Jewish believers tempted to lapse back into the externals of Judaism?

He tied in what they already knew with the new info

Your response

13. What aspect of 3:1-6 would you like to concentrate on for application this week?

_____

_____

_____

_____

_____

14. What difference would you like this truth to make to your life?

_____

_____

_____

_____

_____

15. How can you go about taking this insight to heart and putting it into practice?

_____

_____

_____

_____

_____

_____

Study Skill—Application

The ends of lessons 2 through 4 have given you a framework for planning an application that you can use for Bible study without a study guide: choose a relevant truth; decide how it is relevant or how you want it to affect you; commit yourself to at least one simple step toward acting on the truth you chose.

---

16. List any questions you have about 3:1-6.

_____

_____

_____

_____

For the group

Warm-up. Take five or ten minutes to let everyone share how his or her efforts at application are going. What obstacles and benefits have you encountered as you have tried to meditate on particular verses and do what they say? How can you help each other grow in the areas you have identified as being important to you?

Read aloud and summarize.

Questions. You might focus your attention on the "if" clause in 3:6. What are some practical ways of "holding on" to the courage and hope of which the author speaks? How can you fix your thoughts on Jesus? Hebrews 11:1 points out how faith relates to holding on to courage and hope.

Alternatively, you can explore the difference it makes to each of you that Christ is your apostle and high priest.

Summarize.

Prayer. Praise Jesus for being your apostle and high priest, the builder of everything, and the faithful Son over God's house. Spend some time fixing your thoughts on Him in worship. Ask Him to help you hold on to your courage and hope.

Types

A *type* is a person, event, or thing in the Old Testament that foreshadows a person, event or thing in the New. The type resembles its New Testament *antitype* in some essential feature.[3] Moses was a type of Christ in certain ways:

1. As infants, both were threatened by cruel

(continued on page 50)

(continued from page 49)
rulers and narrowly escaped dying under the rulers' decrees to exterminate Jewish babies (Exodus 1:22, 2:1-10; Matthew 2:13-17).

2. Both mediated between God and His people (Exodus 32:30-32, 1 Timothy 2:5-6).

3. Moses brought the Law written on stone; Jesus brought the Law of the Spirit written on human hearts (Exodus 19:1-20:22, 2 Corinthians 3:3).

4. Both were God's instruments to liberate His people from slavery (Exodus 12:1-35, Colossians 1:13-14).

1. John F. MacArthur, *The MacArthur New Testament Commentary: Hebrews* (Chicago: Moody Press, 1983), page 75.
2. Erich von Eicken and Helgo Lindner, "Apostle," *The New International Dictionary of New Testament Theology*, volume 1, edited by Colin Brown (Grand Rapids, Michigan: Zondervan Corporation, 1975), page 128.
3. William G. Moorehead, "Type," *The International Standard Bible Encyclopedia*, volume 4, edited by Geoffrey Bromiley (Grand Rapids, Michigan: William B. Eerdmans Publishing Company, 1980), page 3029.

LESSON FIVE

HEBREWS 3:7-19

Warning Against Unbelief

"We are his house, if we hold on to our courage and the hope of which we boast" (3:6). And if we don't hold on to our courage and hope? The author answers by quoting Psalm 95, which recalled the familiar story of the Israelites' faithlessness after their deliverance from Egypt.

Read 3:7-19 at least twice, once silently and once aloud. Ask the Holy Spirit to speak to you through these words.

1. The author has demonstrated Christ's superiority over the prophets (1:1-4), the angels (1:5-2:18), and Moses (3:1-6). What, then, is the significance of beginning 3:7-19 with "so"?

   To point out that since Christ is superior, we can certainly trust Him & musn't harden our hearts

2. How does a person "hear his voice" (3:7)? See 1:2.

   listening - quiet time reading his word. Drawing near - James Be spirit minded + spirit led.

For Thought and Discussion:
a. Hebrews 3:7-11 quotes Psalm 95, which many believe to have been penned by David. Yet who is credited with the authorship of this psalm in Hebrews 3:7? *The Holy Spirit*
   b. What does this tell you about Scripture? (Compare 2 Peter 1:21.) *men from God by the Holy Spirit*
   c. How does mentioning this author's name add weight to the warning in Hebrews? *It's from God Himself*

For Further Study:
Why does God issue warnings to His people (Ezekiel 33:11, 2 Peter 3:9)? *He doesn't want anyone to perish*

51

For Further Study:
On how the heart
becomes hard toward
God, see Exodus
8:15; 2 Chronicles
36:13; Nehemiah
9:17; Jeremiah 5:3;
Daniel 5:20; Zecha-
riah 7:12; Mark 3:5-6,
8:17, 16:14. How is
hardness related to
sin?

3. How might the Hebrew believers harden their
   hearts after hearing God's voice? What actions
   and attitudes might this involve?

   unbelief, turning
   away.

Tested (3:9). The Israelites repeatedly tested God by
  questioning whether He was really "among"
  them. When they found themselves without
  water at Massah, for instance, they grumbled
  because they doubted both His ability and His
  willingness to take care of them (Exodus
  17:1-7).

Angry (3:10). Vexed, wrought up, incensed. The
  word is a strong one, "expressive of a strong
  displeasure, amounting to offense."[1]

Known (3:10). Not a mere intellectual knowledge,
  but a knowledge gained by experience. This
  kind of knowledge comes through interacting
  with the ways and character of God.

Rest (3:11). A key Old Testament concept. It meant
  "security from disruption or enemy attack on
  land which has been given as an inheritance
  (Deuteronomy 12:9-10)."[2] Rest was a sign of
  God's presence (Exodus 33:14) and provision
  (Joshua 1:13). Like all the blessings God promises Israel, rest was forfeited if the people sinned
  (Deuteronomy 28:1-68).
  Joshua gave Israel temporary, limited, but
  real rest from its enemies (Joshua 21:44, 22:4,
  23:1). But because the people fell into idolatry
  and other disobedience after Joshua's death,
  Israel suffered repeatedly from attack and inse-

curity for several hundred years (Judges 2:6-23). When David became king and led Israel to be loyal to the Lord, the nation enjoyed rest again (2 Samuel 7:1). Under godly kings after him there was rest (1 Kings 5:4; 2 Chronicles 14:2-6, 20:30), but the bad kings were responsible for sin, internal disorder and discontent, and ultimately national destruction and exile.

According to Psalm 95:7-11, the wilderness generation failed to enter God's rest in Canaan because they faithlessly tested God's power and love at Meribah and Massah (Exodus 17:1-7, Numbers 20:1-13). Hebrews 3:7-4:11 applies this psalm and the story of Joshua to Christians, and shows us how the idea of rest applies to us. Jesus also talked about rest (Matthew 11:28-29).

Study Skill—Word Studies

The above definition of "rest" was composed in two steps that you can follow yourself in study on your own:

1. Look up the word in an exhaustive concordance (see page 182). Then read the verses listed under the word. Examine them in context (you might want to read several paragraphs) to see what is said about the topic. Jot notes.

2. Look up the word in a Bible dictionary, encyclopedia, or commentary. Think about what light the definition there sheds on what you've learned from tracing the word through the Bible.

---

11 Thess 1:7

4. How did the Israelites fail God in the wilderness (3:8-9)?

hardened their hearts, rebelled, tested & tried God, grumbled, complained, doubted,

53

For Further Study:
How does sin cause a heart to become hard and callous, desensitized to the things of God? (See Psalms 17:10, 73:7, 119:70; Matthew 13:15; Acts 28:27.)

Optional Application: Do you see any signs of unbelief in the way you think and act? What practical steps can you take to avoid letting your heart become hard? Develop as specific a "preventive maintenance plan" as possible.

For Thought and Discussion: Why is it so easy to fall prey to sin's deceit (Jeremiah 17:9)?

5. How did God respond to Israel's failure (3:10-11)? (*Optional:* See Deuteronomy 1:34-6, 2:14-15.)

He was angry. He didn't allow them to enter His rest - let alone the promised land.

6. Summarize Hebrews 3:7-11 in terms of cause (3:8-9) and effect (3:10-11).

The hardening of their hearts caused them to not enter God's rest.

See to it (3:12). NASB: "Take care." The idea is "be seeing to it constantly," "keep a watchful eye ever open."

Heart (3:12). We think of the heart as the seat of the emotions, but the Hebrews thought of it as the core of a person—emotions, intellect, and will. The heart is the wellspring of motivation. When the author speaks of the heart believing something, he is talking about deep convictions held in the core of one's being, the beliefs that really determine what one does. Likewise, to harden one's heart is to make one's will, intellect, and emotions all insensitive to God's presence and truth.

Turns away (3:12). Stands aloof or maintains a distance from.

Encourage (3:13). "The root meaning has to do with coming alongside to give help. The writer is saying . . . 'Get alongside each other and help each other.'"[3] Depending on what the situation calls for, encouragement can be a gentle word,

54

a hug, practical help, or a kick in the pants. Yet it is always done from alongside, never condescendingly.

Deceitfulness (3:13). Trickery, strategem. Sin seldom appears as it really is, but usually masks itself.

Share in Christ (3:14). To belong to Christ and participate in the blessings that go along with this relationship.

7. What is the connection between sin and unbelief (3:12-13)?

unbelief leads to sin - also unbelief keeps us from recognizing & repenting of sin — a vicious circle

8. How does 3:16-19 provide a concrete example of this connection?

Their unbelief caused them to rebel & sin.
to rebel & sin

9. In view of the seriousness of the warning in 3:7-12, why is it so important to encourage one another daily (3:13)? What might happen if we fail to encourage one another?

When we're alone & isolate & are not exhorted & encouraged, we tend more to unbelief & sin

Optional Application: How important is it to you that you have come to share in Christ? What practical difference has this made to your life already? What further difference would you like it to make in the way you think and act? How can you respond this week?

For Thought and Discussion: At Kadesh Barnea, the Israelites sinned by repudiating Moses and Aaron, their acting apostle and high priest (Numbers 14:1-45). This was essentially a revolt against God, since He appointed these men to their positions of leadership. Why would a revolt against Jesus be an even worse rebellion with worse consequences?

For Further Study: a. Do godly men ever experience unbelief (see Genesis 17:17, Numbers 11:21-22, Matthew 17:19-20, Luke 24:11)? What is your response to this?
b. Is there a difference between the unbelief in these examples and the kind God condemns? How and to what extent, or why not?

For Thought and Discussion: a. Why is it important to live "Today"? (See Psalm 39:4-5, James 4:14.)
b. How can you go about doing this?

Optional Application: How can you encourage someone today or this week?

For Further Study: a. On how God expresses displeasure when people sin, see Numbers 11:1; Psalm 2:5; 60:1; Zechariah 1:2,15.
b. Is Jesus the same way? (See John 2:14-16.) What are the implications of this for you?

10. If a person has come to "share in Christ," what outward evidence will he show (3:14)?

confidence in Christ

11. What point is the author making by repeating "Today" in 3:7,13,15?

If you wait It may be too late

12. Why do you think this emphasis on "Today" is so important?

It is more difficult to do things when you put them off. Your heart may become more hardened.

13. Verse 19 states the ultimate reason why the Israelites perished in the wilderness. How should this motivate the Hebrew readers to respond to their distressing circumstances?

Trust God + believe He is for them + will take care of them.

Your response

For Further Study:
Add 3:7-19 to your outline. Consider main divisions at 3:7-11, 3:12-15, and 3:16-19.

Study Skill—Application

Asking yourself the following five questions may help you identify issues for application in a passage:

> Is there a *sin* for me to avoid?
> Is there a *promise* for me to trust?
> Is there an *example* for me to follow?
> Is there a *command* for me to obey?
> How can this add to my personal *knowledge* of the Lord (not just knowledge about Him)?

You can remember these questions with the acronym SPECK—Sin, Promise, Example, Command, Knowledge.

Optional Application: Are any circumstances in your life fostering an attitude of unbelief toward God? If so, what have you learned from 3:7-19 that might help you deal with this?

14. What one sin, promise, example, command, or truth about God would you like to concentrate on for application this week?

   I want to trust God enough to keep from testing Him.

15. How would you like this to affect your life?

   more single minded in listening to God.

16. What steps can you take during the next week to begin putting this into practice?

57

_____

_____

_____

17. List any questions you have about 3:7-19.

_____

_____

_____

_____

For the group

Warm-up. Ask, "What have you heard God's voice
say to you today?" Some group members may legit-
imately feel they haven't heard anything. The
important thing here is to acknowledge honestly
where you are. If you haven't heard, it may be that
you are not listening, or it may be that God has
truly been silent today. You can deal with what you
should do about what you have heard or not heard
when you discuss application.

Questions. One action you can take to help keep
each other from being hardened by sin's deceitfulness is to encourage each other. What encouragement can you offer each other today? How can you
make your group a place where encouragement
happens naturally and frequently?

Prayer. Thank God for bringing each of you to share
in Christ. Thank Him for speaking to you. Ask Him
to help you resist sin's deceitfulness and to trust
Him enough to keep from testing Him.

1. Kenneth S. Wuest, *Wuest's Word Studies*, volume 2 (Grand
   Rapids, Michigan: William B. Eerdmans Publishing Company,
   1980), page 76.
2. E. John Hamlin, *Joshua: Inheriting the Land* (Grand Rapids,
   Michigan: William B. Eerdmans Publishing Company, 1983),
   page 12.
3. MacArthur, page 92.

HEBREWS 4:1-16

Unbelief: Consequences and Cure

The Israelites failed to enter God's rest because they disbelieved, tested, and disobeyed God. What are the implications for us? Chapter 4 begins, "Therefore. . . ."

Read 4:1-16 several times, listening for what God is saying to you.

For Thought and Discussion: What does "Therefore" (4:1) tell you?

1. What four exhortations does the author give his readers in this chapter? (Watch for "Let us. . . .")

4:1 *be careful that none of you be found to have fallen short.*

disciplined focus

4:11 *make every effort to enter that effort rest*

4:14 *Hold firmly to the faith we profess.*

4:16 *approach the throne of grace with confidence so we may receive mercy & find grace to help us in our time of need.*

2. What can you conclude about what the author wants to accomplish in this chapter?

effort & encourage

For Further Study:
Read Psalm 62:1-2
and meditate on the
idea of resting in God
alone. How can you
put this into practice?

For Further Study:
Observe how the term
gospel is used in the
Bible (Isaiah 40:9,
52:7; Mark 1:1; Luke
2:10-11; Acts 8:12;
1 Corinthians 15:1-8;
Revelation 14:6-7).
Notice how the word
is used in different
ways depending on
the context.

Entering Sabbath-rest (4:1-11)

Gospel (4:2). Literally, "good news."

3. Good news was proclaimed in Old Testament
   times, just as in the New (4:2). What good news
   were the Israelites given? (See Exodus 19:3-6.)

   They were born up on Eagles wings -- you will be my treasured possession - a kingdom of priests & a holy nation.

4. Why wasn't this gospel enough to bring the
   Israelites to rest (Hebrews 4:2)?

   They didn't maintain faith.

5. When the author speaks of "his rest" and "my
   rest" (4:1,3,5), he means God's rest. What
   would you say is the primary characteristic of
   God's rest (4:4)?

   not striving - having confidence in God

60

6. The Israelites failed to enter God's rest. But how do we know that the promised rest is still available to those with faith (4:6-9)?

V.9 - There remains, then, a Sabbath rest for the people of God.

Optional Application: Is there any unbelief in your heart? Pray about this.

Optional Application: a. If rest is the benefit of faith in the midst of conflict, is rest a reality in your life? If not, is it blocked by unbelief or disobedience of any kind?

    b. What have you learned from 4:1-16 that might help you enter more fully into God's rest?

Peace with God is salvation/rest submission/rest is the Peace of God

7. The statement that "anyone who enters God's rest also rests from his own work" (4:10) has been interpreted as having a present application, a future application, or both. What do the following cross-references reveal about the rest that is available both now and in the future?

present (Matthew 11:28-30, Romans 5:1-2)

the present - coming to Jesus
the future - peace with God thru Jesus - we rejoice in the hope of the glory of God

future (Revelation 14:13, 21:1-4) _Blessed are the dead in the Lord - - they will rest from their labor._
21 v.14 no more death or mourning or crying or pain God will be with us.

Make every effort (4:11). Exert yourself and make haste to do your very best in this endeavor.

61

For Further Study:
On God's complete knowledge of people, see Psalm 139:7-8; Proverbs 5:21; Jeremiah 16:17, 23:24.

For Further Study:
a. Everything in your life will be "laid bare before the eyes of him to whom we must give account" (4:13). Compare this sobering statement to 1 Corinthians 3:11-15 and 2 Corinthians 5:10.

b. How is the expectation of future judgment relevant to your daily life?

Optional Application: What has the Word of God (perhaps in your study of Hebrews) revealed about your own "thoughts and attitudes of the heart" (4:12)? What should you do about what you have learned?

exposes our hearts
enables our
hearts
critic

The living Word (4:12-13)

Word (4:12). "God's truth was revealed by Jesus (the Incarnate Word; see John 1:1,14), but it has also been given verbally, the word referred to here."[1]

Soul and spirit, joints and marrow (4:12). "The totality and depth of one's being."[2]

8. In what five ways does the author describe the Word of God in 4:12? John 6:63 Isa. 49:2

   living/active, sharper
   than any double-edged
   sword, penetrates even to
   dividing soul + spirit, joints +
   marrow, judges the thoughts
   + attitudes of the heart.
   Acts 5 + 7:304

9. How does the emphasis on the Word of God and His penetrating knowledge in 4:12-13 relate to the discussion of unbelief in the heart (4:1-11)?

   we can find truth in
   the Word. It will also
   uncover what the
   problem is.

10. How does 4:12-13 make you want to respond?

    Study the Word more, +
    ask God to uncover stuff
    ↓ help me to deal with it.

Optional Application: Thank God that "nothing in creation is hidden from God's sight" (4:13), that He knows everything about you yet loves you dearly. How should this truth affect the way you live?

For Thought and Discussion: What sharply distinguishes Jesus from ordinary Jewish priests (4:15)?

The great high priest (4:14-16)

11. Recall what the author has previously said about the high priest (2:17-18, 3:1). What further fact should encourage believers to put their full confidence in this high priest (4:15)?

He has been tempted as we are but without sin so he is able to sympathize with our weaknesses.

Sympathize (4:15). To feel or suffer with.

Mercy (4:16). The withholding of deserved punishment.

Grace (4:16). Undeserved favor. The word here is plural, giving the idea of many manifestations of grace to meet specific needs.

12. Because they have a sympathetic yet sinless high priest, Christians can confidently approach God to obtain mercy and grace (4:16). How would these two things be especially important to believers living under severe stress?

They wouldn't have to bear it alone!

For Further Study:
Add chapter 4 to your outline. Where are the logical paragraph divisions?

13. How does this privilege of approaching the throne of grace relate to entering God's rest?

Rolling burdens over

14. Look back at questions 1 and 2, and summarize 4:1-16 in your own words.

Don't fall short of entering God's rest for we by holding firmly to our faith can't not only enter it but since He is our high priest, approach the

Your response _throne of grace with confidence to find grace + help in_

15. What truth from chapter 4 would you like to _time of need_ take to heart this week?

16. How would you like to grow in this area?

64

17. What steps can you take along these lines this week?

_____

_____

_____

_____

_____

_____

18. List any questions you have about 4:1-16.

_____

_____

_____

_____

For the group

Warm-up. Ask, "To what extent do you experience rest in your life?" Have those who answer explain what they mean by rest and how they do or don't experience it.

Questions. Focus on the connection between God's promise of rest (what is it?), how one attains rest, the Word of God, and Jesus as our sympathetic high priest. Also, discuss how you can practice each of the exhortations you listed in question 1.

Prayer. Thank God for His promise of rest both now and in eternity. Ask Him to help you hear His voice and live in His rest. Thank Him for knowing everything about you yet loving you utterly, and for giving you a high priest who fully understands your weaknesses. Go to the Father for mercy and grace to meet your specific needs.

1. The NIV Study Bible, edited by Kenneth Barker (Grand Rapids, Michigan: Zondervan Corporation, 1985), page 1863.
2. The NIV Study Bible, page 1863.

HEBREWS 5:1-10

Superior Priestly Qualifications

We ran into the idea of Jesus as high priest in 4:14-16. In one way or another, chapters 5 through 10 all deal with Jesus' high priesthood—it is one of the central concepts the author wants to get across. Any Hebrew knew what a high priest was, but it was ingrained in him that only a descendant of Aaron could be one. Read 5:1-10, observing what a high priest is and why, despite his ancestry, Jesus is supremely qualified to be one.

1. Running through 5:1-10 is the idea of Christ as the high priest. What is the main idea of each of the following paragraphs?

   5:1-3 _____

   _____

   _____

   5:4-6 _____

   _____

   _____

   5:7-10 _____

   _____

   _____

For Further Study:
On the gifts and sacrifices offered to God for men's sins (Hebrews 5:1), read the first seven chapters of Leviticus, which give a good overview of the five main kinds of sacrifices.

For Further Study:
See Exodus 32:22-24 for an example of a high priest showing he was subject to weakness.

For Further Study:
a. What provisions did the Law make for those who went astray through ignorance (Numbers 15:28)?
b. How did the Law deal with those who intentionally sinned (Numbers 15:30-31)?

2. What two primary duties are expected of every high priest (5:1)?

_____

_____

_____

_____

Deal gently (5:2). "This is the capacity to moderate one's feelings to avoid the extremes of cold indifference and uncontrolled sadness."[1] The word carries the idea of forbearance and magnanimity.

Subject to (5:2). The root of this word literally means "to be lying around." The high priest has weakness in the sense that infirmities and sinful tendencies are lying around him or encircling him. That is, he has a sinful human nature.

Those who are ignorant and are going astray (5:2). This phrase is more literally translated, "those who go astray through ignorance."

3. Since human high priests are "subject to weakness," what effect does this have on their attitude toward others (5:2)?

_____

_____

_____

4. As a high priest, Jesus was not "subject to weakness" like the descendants of Aaron. How, then, could He "deal gently with those who are ignorant and are going astray"? (Recall 2:17-18, 4:15.)

_____

_____

_____

_____

_____

5. Does Jesus have "to offer sacrifices for his own sins, as well as for the sins of the people" (5:3)? Why or why not? (See 4:15, 7:27.)

_____

_____

6. Why do you think high priests must be called by God (5:4)?

_____

_____

_____

_____

_____

7. In Hebrews 5:5-6, the author quotes Psalms 2:7 and 110:4. In these passages, the Father appoints Jesus not merely to a temporary, human high priesthood. What titles does the Father give Jesus?

Psalm 2:6 _____

Psalm 2:7 _____

Psalm 110:4 _____

8. Read Genesis 14:18, and observe what two offices Melchizedek held. How is he an appropriate type (foreshadow, prefigurement) of Christ?

_____

_____

_____

_____

_____

For Further Study:
For more on sacrifices for the sins of the people, see Leviticus 16:15-17; Hebrews 7:27, 9:7. In what ways do the Old Testament sacrifices prefigure the work of Christ on the cross? What are the most significant differences between the two?

For Further Study:
a. High priests must be called by God, just as Aaron was (Hebrews 5:4). Read about Aaron's calling in Exodus 28:1-5.
b. Read about the calling of later high priests in Numbers 20:22-29, 25:10-13.

For Thought and Discussion: What does question 9 teach you about how God hears and answers prayers?

For Thought and Discussion: Psalm 22 speaks prophetically of Christ on the cross. How does Psalm 22:24 relate to the statement that Jesus' prayer "was heard" (Hebrews 5:7)?

Prayers and petitions (5:7). In the garden of Gethsemane (Luke 22:41-44).

Save him from death (5:7). This phrase is better translated "save him *out of* death."

9. Jesus prayed with tears to the One who could save Him out of death, and He "was heard" (5:7). In what sense did the Father answer Jesus' Gethsemane prayer "no," and in what sense did He answer "yes"?

no (Matthew 27:45-50) _____

_____

_____

_____

_____

yes (Matthew 28:1-7) _____

_____

_____

_____

_____

10. How did Jesus show "reverent submission" (5:7)? (See Mark 14:35-36.)

_____

_____

_____

_____

_____

Learned . . . suffered (5:8). A play on words in Greek. Jesus learned (*emathen*) obedience from what He suffered (*epathen*).

11. Though Jesus was the eternal Son of God, He nevertheless "learned obedience from what he suffered" (5:8). This does not imply that before His suffering He was tainted by the sin of disobedience. Yet how did suffering unto death teach Jesus to *know* obedience in a way He couldn't have otherwise?

_____

_____

_____

_____

_____

Made perfect (5:9). The basic idea of this word involves bringing a person or thing to the goal fixed by God. It is used of Jesus in the sense of completing the qualification course for becoming an eternal high priest.

12. Why was obedience amid suffering part of Jesus' qualification course for becoming our high priest? (Recall 4:15, 5:2.)

_____

_____

_____

_____

_____

13. As an eternal high priest, Christ achieved eternal atonement and salvation (5:9). Why is this salvation available only to those who "obey him"?

_____

_____

_____

Optional Application: Praise and thank God for the suffering Jesus went through on your behalf. Also, thank Him that because of what He endured, He is an eternal high priest who understands your every need and problem. How can you respond actively to these truths?

For Further Study: Relate the phrase "he learned obedience from what he suffered" to John 4:34, 5:30, 6:38, 8:28-29. Was Jesus ever disobedient?

71

**Optional
Application:** Christ,
who was obedient to
the Father, calls all
those who follow Him
to obedience (5:8-9).
Are there any areas of
your life in which you
are aware of some
level of disobedience
to God? If so, what
steps can you take
this week to turn
things around?

14. How does this need to obey relate to the temptation of the Hebrews to lapse from Christianity back into the externals of Judaism?

_____

_____

_____

_____

These Hebrew believers were probably suffering religious persecution from the Jewish leaders (especially the high priest, who had the authority to put defecting Jews in jail). By asserting that Jesus was "designated by God to be high priest in the order of Melchizedek," the author set a choice before them as to which high priest would receive their allegiance.

Your response

15. What aspect of 5:1-10 seems most personally relevant to you?

_____

_____

_____

_____

16. How would you like this truth to affect your life?

_____

_____

_____

17. What action can you take in response to this truth this week?

_____

_____

_____

_____

_____

18. List any questions you have about 5:1-10.

_____

_____

_____

_____

For the group

Warm-up. Ask everyone to think of one way in which he or she has gone astray from God's perfect will this week. No one need answer aloud unless someone wishes to. Calling to mind some sin should put you in the proper frame of mind to think about how your eternal high priest deals gently with those who are going astray.

Questions. Ask everyone to share what he or she has learned about Christ as high priest, and how that knowledge should affect his or her day-to-day living. For instance, how does it relate to your daily commitment to holiness, or to those occasions when you fall into sin?

Prayer. Thank God for your gentle high priest who represents you before the Father. Confess sins that are currently burdening you. Offer up petitions with reverent submission, knowing that God will hear you as He heard Jesus. Thank Him for teaching you obedience through your circumstances.

Old Testament Sacrifices

"Gifts and sacrifices" under the old covenant may be classified as follows:

1. **Propitiatory offerings.** These were required when an Israelite became ceremonially unclean or unintentionally sinned against God or his neighbor. There were two types.

a. *Sin offerings* were presented for ritual cleansing, unintentional sins against God, and festivals (especially the Day of Atonement). An animal bore the death penalty the sinner had earned.

b. *Guilt offerings* were a means of making restitution when social, religious, or ritual expectations had not been observed (such as in theft or cheating).

2. **Dedicatory offerings.** These were ways of expressing homage to God. They were not accepted unless the offerers had first presented the required propitiatory offerings. There were three types.

a. *Burnt offerings* symbolized the worshiper's total dedication of himself to God. The sacrificed animal (representing the worshiper) was wholly consumed in fire to depict this.

b. *Grain offerings* expressed thankfulness to God for providing grain. The Hebrew word for this means "gift" or "tribute."

c. *Drink offerings* were meant to give pleasure to God.

3. **Communal offerings.** These followed and complemented the other offerings. There were two types.

a. *Fellowship offerings* (or "peace offerings") celebrated fellowship or peace between God and man, and between man and neighbor. Part of the animal was burnt for God, and parts were eaten by the priests and worshipers in a communal meal. The Hebrew name means "peace" or "well-being."

b. *Voluntary offerings* were responses to God's goodness.

This complex system taught Israel the gravity of sin and the grace of God in providing ways to deal with sin on a regular basis. It also made

(continued on page 75)

(continued from page 74)
the point that man must know what God deserves from him and respond accordingly. Notice the progression: sin is dealt with; the cleansed person dedicates himself and his possessions wholly to God; the worshiper and God celebrate fellowship.

These gifts and sacrifices were a temporary measure. They "were not able to clear the conscience of the worshiper. They are only a matter of food and drink and various ceremonial washings—external regulations applying until the time of the new order" (Hebrews 9:9-10).

1. Zane C. Hodges, "Hebrews," *The Bible Knowledge Commentary*, edited by John F. Walvoord and Roy B. Zuck (Wheaton: Victor Books, 1983), page 791.

HEBREWS 5:11-6:12

Spiritual Degeneration

The writer has just warmed up to discussing Christ's priesthood, but he feels compelled to insert another warning before going further. His readers' immaturity and sluggishness make him wonder how much they can digest. He wants to arouse them to greater attentiveness to this deep truth and at the same time to face the danger of not bothering.

Read 5:11-6:12 at least twice.

For Thought and Discussion: Where does the writer's mood suddenly change in 5:11-6:12? Why is this important?

1. What would you say is the main message of 5:11-6:12?

   Show diligence in persevering in the faith.

Slow to learn (5:11-14)

We have much to say about this (5:11). The discussion of Jesus' Melchizedek priesthood goes on from 7:1 to 10:18.

Slow (5:11). A combination of two Greek words meaning "no" and "push." The compound word

77

Optional Application: Evaluate your present level of spiritual maturity based on the marks in 5:11-14. Pray about what you should do about what you learn.

Optional Application: a. How can you improve in your ability to use God's Word as a standard by which to distinguish good from evil?

b. How can you practice using God's Word for discernment this week? Think of at least one decision you are facing that requires discernment.

means "sluggish," "slow," or "numb." When used of people, it usually indicates intellectual numbness or thickness. (NASB: "dull of hearing.")

2. What are the spiritual deficiencies of this group of Hebrew believers (5:11-14)?

dull of hearing
sluggish, lazy
can't discern good + evil

3. According to 5:11-14, what are the primary marks of spiritual maturity?

using gifts growing
discerning good + evil
share truth

Not acquainted (5:13). Inexperienced or unskilled—unable to put information to effective use.

Distinguish good from evil (5:14). The ability to discern what is morally good or doctrinally correct from what is contrary to law (divine or human) or truth. The idea is akin to the sense of taste, by which a child grows through practice to distinguish spinach from ice cream and good food from spoiled.

4. a. What does the author mean by "solid food" (5:12,14)?

78

_____

_____

_____

b. Why is "solid food" only for the mature? Why can't infant Christians handle it?

_____

_____

_____

_____

_____

For Thought and Discussion: How might the Hebrew believers have been failing to train themselves to distinguish good from evil?

Optional Application: How are you doing on training yourself to distinguish good from evil? What steps can you take to improve in this area?

5. How does a person train himself to distinguish good from evil? Explain in your own words.

_____

_____

_____

_____

_____

Pressing on (6:1-3)

Leave (6:1). Forsake, put away, let alone, disregard. This word indicates a total detachment or separation from a previous location or condition.

Elementary teachings (6:1). When used of language, this phrase refers to the letters of the alphabet as the basic parts of words—the ABCs. Here it refers to the ABCs of doctrine.

The six elementary teachings in 6:1-2 are doctrines found in both the Old and New Testaments. They constitute a common ground between Judaism and Christianity. Judaism taught that sinners must repent, that converts from paganism must be baptized to symbolize being cleansed from defilement, and that one

For Further Study:
Using a concordance, research Old Testament references to repentance, washing from sin, faith, resurrection ("rise"), and judgment.

For Thought and Discussion: When the author says, "And God permitting, we will do so" (6:3), what in 6:1 is he referring to?

must have faith in God. Jews laid hands on the sick for healing, on new converts, and on missionaries and emissaries for commissioning. They expected a bodily resurrection of the dead and divine judgment at the end of the age.

Because of the similarities between the Jewish and Christian understanding of these doctrines, this group of Hebrew believers may have reasoned that they were not really deserting Christianity by lapsing back into the externals of Judaism. The essence of the author's argument is that the one difference between the two faiths—Jesus Christ—is crucial.

Acts that lead to death (6:1). Literally, "dead works," probably a reference to the Old Testament priestly rituals. They were lifeless because they were incapable of imparting the eternal life available in Christ.

6. What does "Therefore" (6:1) refer back to? (What is the connection between 5:11-14 and 6:1-3?)

_____

_____

_____

_____

_____

A sober warning (6:4-8)

Study Skill—Hermeneutics
Hermeneutics is the science of interpretation. Through this science, Bible scholars try to interpret the meaning of the Bible as accurately as possible. One primary hermeneutical principle is that "obscure passages must give way to clear passages."[1] This means that when a difficult passage is encountered in the Bible, it must be interpreted in light of
(continued on page 81)

(continued from page 80)
what other clear and easier passages say about this issue. Whatever the difficult passage may mean, it must agree with what the clear and easier passages teach. This principle is invaluable for studying the warning passages in Hebrews.

Hebrews 6:4-6 is especially difficult. On page 86 is a careful, extended approach to studying this passage in depth as an exercise in hermeneutics. Tackle it if you have the time and desire.

For Thought and Discussion: How would lapsing back into the externals of Judaism subject Christ to public disgrace and in effect crucify Him again (6:6)?

It is impossible (6:4-6). Scholars have understood this warning in three ways:

1. Christians can actually lose their salvation by walking away from Christ, and it is impossible to be saved a second time.

2. These verses refer to professing believers, not genuine ones. Verses 4-5 describe experiences that fall short of salvation.

3. This passage portrays a hypothetical situation. If a Christian could hypothetically lose his salvation, then there would be no further provision for repentance.

The coming age (6:5). The Jewish way of referring to the Kingdom of God or eternal life (Mark 10:30).

Fall away (6:6). To deviate from the right path. Some people think the writer is talking about falling away from salvation, others from Christian maturity.

7. Why is it impossible to bring those who have fallen away "back to repentance" (6:6)?

_____

_____

_____

_____

81

For Further Study:
God's anger against sinful people is often likened to the burning of fire. See Isaiah 9:18-19, 10:17; Hebrews 10:27, 12:29.

Burned (6:8). It was common in biblical times to burn a field to destroy weeds, thorns, and thistles in order to enable a farmer to re-cultivate the land. Verses 7-8 are a parable illustrating verses 4-6.

8. How are maturing, committed Christians like the land in 6:7?

9. How are those who fall away like the land in 6:8?

10. What do you think is the essential point the author wants to get across in 6:4-8?

82

Diligence to the end (6:9-12)

11. Does the author actually expect his readers to suffer the fate of the worthless land (6:9-10)? What does he expect, and why?

_____

_____

_____

_____

_____

12. Why does helping God's people show love to Him (6:10)?

_____

_____

_____

_____

_____

13. What is the author's desire (6:11)?

_____

_____

_____

_____

Lazy (6:12). The same Greek word rendered "slow" in 5:11. It again suggests "sluggish."

14. How is the laziness mentioned in 6:12 related to 5:11-14?

_____

_____

For Thought and Discussion: What are some "things that accompany salvation" (6:9-10)?

Optional Application: One practical sign of a Christian's love for God is his commitment to helping God's people (6:10). How can you show love for God in this way this week? Pray for and act on one concrete way of doing this.

83

Optional Application: Thank God for the eternal inheritance you have been promised (6:12). How does this expectation motivate you to act today?

Optional Application: How can you show faith and patience in your current circumstances?

For Further Study: Even if you have not been making outlines of every passage, give 5:11-6:12 a try. Let your main divisions be 5:11-14, 6:1-3, 6:4-6, 6:7-8, 6:9-12.

15. Practically speaking, how can the persecuted Hebrew Christians imitate their faithful and patient predecessors (6:12)? (What aspects of their circumstances call for faith and patience?)

16. Now that you've studied 5:11-6:12 more closely, reread your answer to question 1, and refine your summary of the passage if necessary.

Your response

17. What one aspect of 5:11-6:12 would you like to take to heart this week?

18. How would you like this to affect your life?

84

19. What concrete step(s) can you take to begin letting this happen?

_____

_____

_____

_____

_____

20. List any questions you have about 5:11-6:12.

_____

_____

_____

_____

For the group

Warm-up. Take a few minutes to share how your efforts at application have gone during the past two weeks. How have you been able to put into practice what you have been learning? What obstacles, if any, have you encountered?

Questions. You could easily spend two meetings on 5:11-6:12, especially if you choose to wrestle with 6:4-8. These verses have caused some Christians to fear that they may lose their salvation through some sin. This fear has caused many to lose spiritual joy and confidence in their Savior, and so to become unfruitful through despair. If anyone in your group has such feelings, discuss why this is exactly the wrong response to 6:4-8, regardless of whether you think it is theoretically possible for a real believer to lose his or her salvation. Make sure everyone understands that the author's purpose—far from sowing despair—is to motivate his readers to faith and patience.

We've made a detailed study of 6:4-6 optional so as not to bog down anyone who wants to move more quickly. You can decide as a group whether to tackle this.

Prayer. Thank God for enlightening you, for letting you taste the heavenly gift, for bringing you to share in the Holy Spirit, and for giving you a taste of the goodness of the Word of God and the powers of the coming age. Ask Him to strengthen you to face your circumstances with faith and patience, so that you will produce a fruitful crop and continue to show love toward His people.

Falling Away

If you want to delve into 6:4-6 deeply to decide what the author is really getting at here, consider the following questions.

1. In 6:1-3, the writer uses the pronouns "us" and "we." In 6:4-6 he uses "those" and "they." Then he switches back to "us" and "we" in 6:9-12.

   a. Who are "we" in 6:1-3?

   b. Who are "they" in 6:4-6? (Are "they" different from "we"?) How can you tell?

   c. What do you think is the significance of this switch from "we" to "they"? (Does it suggest that the author is talking about a hypothetical situation? Why or why not?)

2. a. By what four phrases does the writer describe the "they" group in 6:4-5?

   b. Do these four phrases indicate to you that the author is talking about genuine born-again Christians? Why or why not? (*Optional:* See Romans 6:23, 8:9; 2 Corinthians 4:3-6; Ephesians 2:8; Hebrews 2:9; 1 Peter 1:23; Jude 19.)

3. Do you think "falling away" in 6:6 refers to falling from salvation or from maturity? Why?

4. Can a true believer fall away from salvation? What do Jesus and Paul say about this in John 6:39-40, 10:27-30; Romans 8:31-39?

1. Bernard Ramm, *Protestant Biblical Interpretation: A Textbook of Hermeneutics* (Grand Rapids, Michigan: Baker Book House, 1978), page 104.

HEBREWS 6:13-20

God's Promise Certain

We must "imitate those who through faith and patience inherit what has been promised" (6:12). But who are those? The supreme Old Testament example is Abraham. And why should we patiently trust the promise? Read 6:13-20 at least twice, asking yourself this question.

1. What words or concepts occur over and over again in 6:13-20?

_____

_____

_____

_____

_____

2. What seems to be the main goal or message of this passage?

_____

_____

_____

_____

_____

For Thought and
Discussion: a. Part
of God's promise to
Abraham was that
"through your off-
spring all nations on
earth will be blessed"
(Genesis 22:18). How
have all the nations
on earth been blessed
through Abraham's
offspring (Matthew
1:1)?

b. Did Abraham
see this promise ful-
filled? (See Hebrews
11:13.)

c. What does this
tell you about waiting
patiently on God and
His promises?

Optional
Application: How
can you follow Abra-
ham's example of
waiting patiently for
the fulfillment of
promises?

Abraham's patience rewarded (6:13-15)

Abraham (6:13). Jews esteemed him as the father of their race and the paramount example of faith.

After waiting patiently (6:15). When Abraham was seventy-five years old, God promised to make him into a great nation (Genesis 12:1-4). For the next twenty-five years, Abraham's wife continued to be barren. At last Sarah bore Isaac, and the promise was fulfilled (Genesis 21:5). But when Isaac was a teenager, God told Abraham to offer him as a sacrifice to demonstrate his loyalty to God (Genesis 22:1-2). When Abraham proved he was willing to do even this, God stayed his hand and said, "I swear by myself, declares the LORD, that because you have done this and have not withheld your son, your only son, I will surely bless you and make your descendants as numerous as the stars in the sky . . ." (Genesis 22:16-18).

3. What does Abraham's life show about the meaning of waiting patiently for what God has promised? (*Optional:* Read Genesis 12:1-4; 15:1-6; 17:1-7,15-22; 21:1-5; 22:1-18.)

_____

_____

_____

_____

_____

_____

Anchor for the soul (6:16-22)

Oath (6:16). "When men swear an oath in order to underline the certainty and solemnity of their words, they swear by someone or something greater than themselves. 'As the Lord liveth' was the supreme oath in Israel. Abraham himself swore by God and made others do the same (Genesis 14:22, 21:23-24, 24:3). But, says our author, God has none greater than Himself by whom to swear."[1]

4. Why did God swear an oath with His promise to bless Abraham and give him descendants (6:16-18)?

_____

_____

_____

_____

_____

For Further Study: See other oaths God has made (Psalms 89:35-37, 95:10-11; Isaiah 14:24-27, 62:8-9). Has God honored these oaths?

For Thought and Discussion: Christians are often spoken of as heirs (Romans 8:17, Galatians 3:29, Titus 3:7). What does it mean to you personally that you possess an eternal inheritance that is secure for you in heaven?

Puts an end to all argument (6:16). This idea is rooted in Old Testament Law. Exodus 22:10-11, for instance, says that an oath will settle a dispute between two parties when no proof is available on either side.

Unchangeable (6:18). The Greeks often used this term regarding one's last will and testament. Once a will was properly made, it was unchangeable by anyone but the maker. God has declared that His promise and oath to Abraham is unchangeable, even by Himself.

5. What are the "two unchangeable things" (6:18) that together provide a double assurance that God won't retract His promise?

_____

_____

_____

_____

_____

For Further Study:
Unless we can have
total confidence in
God's veracity, His
promises are little
comfort. Research
God's reliability in
John 1:14,17; 3:33;
14:6,16-17; 15:26;
16:13; 17:17.

6. The sworn promise to give heirs to Abraham is one promise we can be sure God will not retract. But this is not the promise the author means to focus on. What other sworn promise is he talking about (Hebrews 5:6, 6:20; Psalm 110:4)?

_____

_____

_____

_____

7. Who are the "heirs" (6:17) of both the promise to Abraham and the one in Psalm 110:4?

_____

_____

8. What "hope" (sure expectation) do these promises give to Christians?

_____

_____

_____

_____

9. Why should this hope have been such a source of encouragement to Christians under persecution for their faith (6:18)?

_____

_____

_____

_____

10. Why should this hope be an anchor for *your* soul, firm and secure (6:19)?

_____

_____

_____

_____

_____

Fled (6:18). The Greek root means "to flee for refuge." The same root was used for a man who accidently killed his neighbor and fled for refuge to a city where he could be safe from an avenging kinsman (Numbers 35:6-34, Deuteronomy 19:1-14). In Hebrews 6:18 the emphasis is not so much on fleeing *from* something as on fleeing *toward* Jesus.

Anchor (6:19). The harbors were quite shallow in the Mediterranean Sea. Hence, a ship could not enter a harbor when a storm threatened, because the hull would shatter when the ship was tossed in shallow water. Furthermore, the Mediterranean floor was sand without rock, so it would not have provided a secure anchor.

Therefore, to secure a ship, the anchor was put into a shallow boat, this smaller boat was rowed into the harbor, and the anchor was secured to the shore. The author has this scene in mind when he portrays Christ as the forerunner "rowing" into the inner sanctuary and securing the anchor there.

Firm and secure (6:19). "Firm" implies something that cannot be made to totter when put to the test. "Secure" suggests something that does not break down under the weight of a heavy object.

---

11. Why can we be confident that our hope is securely anchored (6:19-20)? (Consider where it is anchored.)

_____

_____

For Thought and Discussion: From what do you think the Hebrew believers "fled" (6:18)?

For Thought and Discussion: Why is it important to you personally that it is impossible for God to lie (Numbers 23:19, Hebrews 6:18)?

Optional Application: How solidly anchored is your hope? If you feel like you are adrift in your spiritual life, what have you learned in this lesson that might help you rectify the situation?

**Optional
Application:** What in
6:13-20 gives you a
sense of personal
security in your rela-
tionship with God?
How can you respond
in action?

**For Thought and
Discussion:** a. If
hope is an anchor for
the soul, what is the
turbulent sea you are
sailing in?
   b. What sea were
the Hebrew Christians
in danger of drifting in
if they lost their
anchor?

**For Thought and
Discussion:** How
does the assurance of
6:13-20 complement
the warning in
6:1-12?

_____

_____

Inner sanctuary (6:19). The Jewish sanctuary had
   two rooms. Priests entered the outer one, the
   Holy Place, daily in performing their duties
   (burning incense, offering prayers, and so on).
   The inner room, the Most Holy Place, was
   closed to all but the high priest, and he could
   enter it only once a year, on the Day of Atonement, with a blood sacrifice for the nation. A
   rope was tied around the high priest's ankle
   when he entered, so that if God rejected the
   sacrifice and struck the priest dead, others
   could remove the body without violating the
   sanctuary.

_____

12. To see that you fully understand the main point
    of 6:13-20, try paraphrasing it in your own
    words.

_____

_____

_____

_____

_____

Your response

13. What aspect of 6:13-20 seems most personally
    significant to you?

_____

_____

_____

_____

_____

14. How would you like this to affect your life?

For Further Study:
Add 6:13-20 to your outline.

15. What steps can you take this week to begin this process, by God's grace?

16. List any questions you have about 6:13-20.

For the group

Warm-up. Ask each person to name one promise God has given him or her. This can be a promise specific to the individual, or a dearly valued scriptural promise.

Questions. Focus on what God's promises are, why you can rely on them, and how you should act while awaiting their fulfillment. Do you act as though you trust God's promises?

Prayer. Thank God for the confidence you can have in His promises. Thank Him for your hope of eternal life, securely anchored in the very throne room of God, into which Jesus has entered. Ask God to help you live daily with patient faith in that hope.

1. Bruce, page 130.

HEBREWS 7:1-28

A Superior Priestly Order

The author started to encourage his readers by explaining what a great high priest Jesus is (4:14-5:10), but he paused because he doubted whether such immature believers could understand about the Melchizedek priesthood. After a warning and exhortation, he now returns to the topic.

Read chapter 7 at least twice, asking the Lord to show you what difference it makes to you that Jesus is your high priest. If you haven't already done so, read Genesis 14:17-20 for background.

For Further Study: Compare Melchizedek's titles to the messianic titles in Isaiah 9:6-7; Jeremiah 23:5-6, 33:15-16.

Who is Melchizedek? (7:1-3)

King . . . and priest (7:1). It was common among the Canaanites for one man to hold both offices (Melchizedek was a Canaanite priest-king in Abraham's day). However, this was expressly forbidden in Israel under the Law of Moses. Priests came from the tribe of Levi, while kings came from Judah.

Salem (7:1). A shortened form of "Jerusalem." *Salem* is related to *shalom*, "peace."

Without genealogy (7:3). Genesis makes a point of recounting the ancestry, birth, and death of almost all of its main characters, but it omits this information in Melchizedek's case.

1. The author has previously used *contrast* (versus prophets, angels, Moses) to make his points about Jesus. Now he uses *comparison*. Below, list all the ways Jesus is like Melchizedek (7:1-3).

Melchizedek	Jesus

The greatness of Melchizedek (7:4-10)

2. Verse 4 says, "Just think how great he was." How does 7:4-10 show Melchizedek's greatness?

7:4-6a _____

_____

_____

7:6b-7 _____

_____

_____

For Further Study:
On the tithes to Levitical priests, see Numbers 18:21-32.

7:8 _____

_____

_____

7:9-10 _____

_____

_____

In the body of his ancestor (7:10). "Levi was Abraham's great-grandson, and was yet unborn when Abraham met Melchizedek; but an ancestor is regarded in biblical thought as containing within himself all his descendants."[1] Also, the Hebrews held that no son (or descendant) could ever be greater than his father (or ancestor), so Levi could not be greater than a man who was his great-grandfather's superior.

3. What is the author's point in proving that the historical Melchizedek was greater than Abraham and Levi?

_____

_____

_____

_____

Jesus like Melchizedek (7:11-28)

Perfection (7:11). Here the word refers to complete and unhindered communion with God.

97

4. a. What did the Levitical priesthood fail to accomplish (7:11)?

_____

_____

_____

_____

b. How do we know it failed (7:11)?

_____

_____

_____

_____

5. Hebrews 7:11,17,20 all cite Psalm 110:4, which
was written midway in the history of the Levitical priesthood (a thousand years before Christ).
What does this tell you about how God already
regarded the Levitical priesthood at that time?

_____

_____

_____

_____

_____

6. The Law of Moses assigned the priesthood to
the tribe of Levi (Deuteronomy 18:1). Why did
the Law have to be changed in order for Jesus
to become high priest in the order of Melchizedek (Hebrews 7:12-14)?

_____

_____

_____

_____

_____

Another priest (7:15). "The Greek language has two words for 'another.' *Allos* means another of the same kind. The word used in verse 15, however, is *heteros*, which means another of a different kind. The first indicates a quantitative difference, the second a qualitative difference."[2] Christ is a high priest of a completely different order than the Levitical one.

Regulation (7:16). The one in the Law that restricted the priesthood to Levi.

For Further Study: Jesus belonged to the tribe of Judah (Matthew 1:1-3; Luke 3:23,33; Revelation 5:5). To learn more about this tribe and its characteristics, use a concordance and look up all the biblical references.

7. What is and is not the basis of Christ's priesthood (7:15-17)?

is _____

_____

is not _____

_____

For Further Study: Hebrews 7:16 alludes to Christ's eternal existence. Read Micah 5:2; John 8:58, 17:5; and Revelation 22:13 to see what they say about this.

Set aside (7:18). Cancel, annul, completely do away with. The Greeks used this word for annulling a treaty, a promise, a law, or a regulation, or for removing a person's name from a legal document.

8. Romans 7:12 says the Law is "holy, righteous, and good." Why, then, does Hebrews 7:18 say the regulation regarding the Levitical priesthood "was weak and useless"?

_____

_____

_____

_____

_____

_____

Our "better hope" enables us to "draw near to God" (7:19). Read 4:16 and 10:22, and think about what you learn about drawing near to God. Can you think of any other passages that talk about this?

Optional Application: How does 7:1-28 help you have confidence to "draw near to God" (7:19)? Meditate on the reasons why you are able to draw near. Then take about fifteen minutes to draw near to God in prayer, enjoying His presence, laying out your concerns, and thanking Him for welcoming you.

9. What is the "better hope" provided by Christ and His priesthood (7:19)?

_____

_____

_____

_____

_____

_____

10. What is the significance of Jesus becoming a priest with an oath (7:20-22)? (Recall 6:13-20.)

_____

_____

_____

_____

_____

Permanent (7:24). Unchangeable, unalterable.

Completely (7:25). To the uttermost, to the ultimate, perfectly, finally and for all time and eternity. (NASB: "forever.")

11. How does Christ's "permanent priesthood" (7:24) relate to His ability "to save completely those who come to God through him" (7:25)?

_____

_____

_____

_____

_____

_____

Intercede (7:25). Literally, "to stand between." Jesus stands astride a chasm between two cliffs, bridging the gap between God and man. He pleads our case before His Father's throne, saying that He has personally paid the price for our rebellious deeds. When as sinners we are unworthy to enter God's presence, Jesus begs the Father's forgiveness on our behalf. He also asks the Father to do for us what He and the Father know is best for us. He is able to fulfill this role as intercessor because He is fully human and fully divine.

12. Jesus is able to save us completely *because* He always lives to intercede for us (7:25). How are the salvation and the intercession connected?

_____

_____

_____

_____

_____

13. Christ's high priesthood is described in five ways in 7:26. How does 7:26-28 contrast Christ's priesthood with the Levitical one?

Christ	Levi

Optional Application: What difference does it make to you that Christ is interceding in heaven on your behalf? Let the implications of this truth sink into you as you meditate on them. How do they affect your perspective on yourself and your situation?

For Further Study:
a. What do you learn about Christ's intercession from Luke 22:31-32, John 17:6-26, Romans 8:33-34, 1 John 2:1?
   b. Is it possible for a person to survive spiritually without Christ interceding for him constantly? Why or why not?

101

For Thought and Discussion: "Once for all" (7:27) is a constant emphasis in Hebrews. Watch for it in 9:12,26; 10:10.

For Thought and Discussion: What signs do you see in 7:23,27 that the high priests appointed under the Law are weak?

For Thought and Discussion: How has the Son "been made perfect" (7:28)? Recall 2:10.

Christ	Levi

14. How would you summarize chapter 7?

_____

_____

_____

_____

_____

Your response

15. What insight from 7:1-28 would you like to concentrate on for application this week?

_____

_____

_____

_____

16. How would you like it to affect your character and approach to life?

_____

102

_____

_____

_____

_____

_____

17. What action can you take to begin putting this
into practice?

_____

_____

_____

_____

_____

**For Thought and
Discussion:** How
does the author's
emphasis on Christ's
superior priesthood
relate to his overall
purpose of keeping
his readers from laps-
ing away?

For Further Study:
Add chapter 7 to your
outline.

18. List any questions you have about 7:1-28.

_____

_____

_____

For the group

Warm-up. Ask everyone to respond to this question:
"If you knew that someone was interceding for you
constantly, what would you like that person to be
praying?" Your answers will probably give you some
new insights into each other and may make you
more aware that Jesus really is interceding for your
deepest needs.

Questions. Discuss the security and assurance chapter 7 is meant to give you. Explore key phrases like
"guarantee of a better covenant" (7:22), "permanent
priesthood" (7:24), "able to save completely" (7:25),
"always lives to intercede" (7:25), "once for all"

(7:27), and "made perfect forever" (7:28). What impact should each of these have on the way you deal with your circumstances and yourselves?

Question 8 is key for understanding the Law. However, it may require more background in Romans than your group has. Consider assigning someone to research how New Testament writers view the Law. Romans 7 is an excellent place to start, and you may also find commentaries on Romans helpful.

Prayer. Praise Jesus for being your holy, blameless, pure, and exalted high priest. Thank Him for guaranteeing your covenant with God, for interceding on your behalf, for saving you completely and forever. Ask Him to help you take on His holy and blameless character, and to live confidently in the assurance of His salvation and intercession. Draw near to God together in confidence.

1. Bruce, page 142.
2. MacArthur, page 190.

HEBREWS 8:1-13

The New Covenant

Christ's priesthood is greater than Aaron's (7:1-28),
bringing "a better hope" (7:19) through "a better
covenant" (7:22). What is this better covenant?
Read 8:1-13 aloud to yourself, looking for what is
new about the new covenant.

1. What is the central point being made in each of
   the following sections?

   8:1-2 _____

   _____

   _____

   8:3-6 _____

   _____

   _____

   _____

   8:7-12 _____

   _____

   _____

   _____

   8:13 _____

   _____

The main point (8:1-2)

2. When the author says "we have such a high priest" (8:1), what kind of high priest is he referring to (7:23-28)?

_____

_____

_____

_____

_____

_____

3. He mentions Christ sitting down at the right hand of God five times (1:3,13; 8:1; 10:12; 12:2). Why? How does this show that Jesus' ministry is superior to that of the Levitical priests (10:11-12)?

_____

_____

_____

_____

_____

_____

True (8:2). Not the opposite of false, but the opposite of shadowy or unreal.

4. Jesus has sat down, but He still serves as priest before the Father (8:2). What is His ongoing priestly service (7:25, 9:24)?

_____

_____

_____

_____

5. What do you learn about the heavenly and earthly tabernacles from 8:2; 9:11,24?

heavenly	earthly

For Thought and Discussion: One of the primary functions of a high priest was to offer sacrifices (8:3). What did Jesus offer (9:14)?

For Thought and Discussion: Why would Jesus not be a priest on earth (8:4)? (Recall 5:1-3, 7:14.)

Copy and shadow (8:3-6)

6. What do the terms "copy," "shadow," and "pattern" indicate to you about the Levitical priesthood (8:5)?

_____

_____

_____

_____

_____

Covenant (8:6). See the box on pages 111-112.

7. Hebrews 8:6 speaks of three new things that are "better" than or "superior" to their former counterparts. How is each better than its predecessor?

107

Optional Application: How should the fact that your relationship to God is based on Jesus' sacrifice, not on working to please God, affect your feelings and actions?

For Thought and Discussion: What was Christ's role as mediator (Galatians 3:20; 1 Timothy 2:5; Hebrews 8:6, 9:15, 12:24; 1 John 2:1)?

Jesus' ministry as high priest (recall 7:11-28)

_____

_____

_____

_____

_____

_____

the new covenant (8:6-13)

_____

_____

_____

_____

_____

the promises on which the covenant is based (8:10-12)

_____

_____

_____

_____

_____

_____

Promises (8:6). The old covenant was founded on conditional promises: "If you obey me fully . . . then . . . you will be my treasured possession" (Exodus 19:5-6; compare Deuteronomy 28:1-2). However, the inner power of the Holy Spirit that enables a person to obey was not given along with the commands.

Old and new (8:7-13)

8. God set the terms of both the old and new covenants. Why did He choose to initiate a new one (8:7-9)?

_____

_____

_____

_____

_____

Remain faithful (8:9). Persevere, hold fast, remain true to. (NASB: "continue in.")

Minds (8:10). One's innermost thoughts and understanding.

9. List the foundational blessings of the new covenant, and explain what they mean (8:10-12).

_____

_____

_____

_____

_____

_____

_____

_____

_____

_____

_____

For Further Study:
Research the idea of God's Law being written on human hearts. See Psalm 37:31, 40:8; Jeremiah 31:33; Romans 2:15, 7:22; 2 Corinthians 3:3; Hebrews 10:16.

For Further Study:
Was knowing God lacking among the Israelites under the old covenant (Judges 2:10; Hosea 4:1,6)? How did they show it?

Optional Application: Meditate on the fact that God has chosen not to remember your sins any more (8:12). How does this motivate you to act? Start by thanking God.

Optional Application: Commit the blessings of the new covenant (8:10-12) to memory. How can you act in light of these truths this week?

For Thought and Discussion: What is involved in knowing God (8:11)? From a human standpoint, how do we make this a concrete reality? (See Jeremiah 9:23-24, John 17:3.)

Know (8:11). The Hebrew idea is knowledge that comes by personal experience.

Aging (8:13). Decaying or waning in strength.

Will soon disappear (8:13). In fact, the Romans demolished the Jewish Temple just a few years after this letter was written, and no orthodox Levitical priest has offered a sacrifice since then.

10. Summarize 8:1-13 in your own words.

_____

_____

_____

_____

_____

Your response

11. What one truth from 8:1-13 would you like to take to heart this week?

_____

_____

_____

_____

12. How would you like this to affect your life?

_____

_____

_____

_____

13. What steps can you take to begin letting this happen?

For Further Study:
Continue your outline of Hebrews with chapter 8.

_____

_____

_____

_____

_____

_____

14. List any questions you have about chapter 8.

_____

_____

_____

_____

For the group

Warm-up. Take a few minutes to let group members share how their efforts to apply Hebrews are going. What difference has your study made to your lives so far? What difficulties have you had in connecting your study with your lives?

Prayer. Thank God for the terms of the new and better covenant. Let each person thank Him especially for the blessings that are most important to him or her.

The Covenant

The Hebrew word for _covenant_ comes from a root that means "to bind." Among the ancient Israelites, a covenant was a relationship between two parties wherein each bound himself to perform a certain service or duty for the other. When two men made such a covenant, they invoked divine retribution if either one tried to avoid fulfilling the covenant obligations. That was how binding such covenants were considered to be.

(continued on page 112)

111

(continued from page 111)

A covenant could be between two equal parties or between unequals. It could be a bilateral agreement (in which two parties made the initiative and agreed on the terms) or a unilateral one (in which one party declared the terms). It could be a pact between friends, a marriage commitment, a political treaty, or a business contract. God's covenant with Israel was unilateral and between unequals. It resembled a treaty between a sovereign and a subject people, and also a marriage. It was an act of unearned grace for the benefit and blessing of the people. God's motive was based on what the Hebrews called *hesed* (lovingkindness, steadfast love, mercy, loyalty, covenant love). The Old Testament uses covenant terminology extensively:

"I will *establish* my covenant with you" (Genesis 6:18).

"I will *confirm* my covenant between me and you" (Genesis 17:2).

"I have *remembered* my covenant" (Exodus 6:5-6).

"I will not reject them . . . *breaking* my covenant with them" (Leviticus 26:44).

"He *declared* to you his covenant" (Deuteronomy 4:13).

"He will not abandon or destroy you or *forget* the covenant with your forefathers, which he *confirmed* to them by *oath*" (Deuteronomy 4:31).

"they have *violated* my covenant" (Joshua 7:11).

Against this backdrop, the author of Hebrews discusses the new covenant first announced by Jeremiah (Jeremiah 31:31-34). This new covenant was a drastic revision of the old one, and its ratification made the old one null and void.

112

HEBREWS 9:1-10

The Earthly Tabernacle

Christ is a greater high priest than Aaron, and the new covenant is better than the old. In chapter 9, the writer goes on to compare the sanctuary and sacrifices of the old covenant to those of the new. Read Hebrews 9:1-10 at least twice.

Furnishings of the tabernacle (9:1-5)

The following notes are provided as background if you are less than familiar with the details of the tabernacle and its furniture. You will find it helpful to read the passages of Exodus cited for each item, but you can omit them if you are pressed for time.

Tabernacle (9:2). The Hebrew counterpart of this Greek word means "dwelling place." After God delivered Israel from Egypt, He commanded the people to build a royal tent to be His dwelling place in their midst and the focus of their worship. God minutely specified the details of the tent's/tabernacle's construction (Exodus 26:1-37). Centuries later, when the Israelites were settled in the promised land, God allowed them to build a permanent temple on the pattern of the moveable tabernacle.

Both the temple and the tabernacle had two rooms, the Holy Place and the Most Holy Place.

Lampstand (9:2). Read Exodus 25:31-40.

Table and the consecrated bread (9:2). Read Exodus 25:23-30. The bread was a thank offering for the provision of daily bread, consecrating the fruit of Israel's labors. Twelve loaves were placed each week in the Holy Place.

Golden altar of incense (9:4). Read Exodus 30:1-10. Incense was burned daily to symbolize the prayers of the people rising fragrantly to God.

Ark of the covenant (9:4). Read Exodus 25:10-16. The old English word *ark* means "chest," as does the Hebrew word in Exodus 25:10-16. It is a different Hebrew word from the one for Noah's ark. The ark of the covenant was a wooden chest in which symbols of the covenant were stored: the *golden jar of manna* (see Exodus 16:32-34); *Aaron's staff* (see Numbers 17:8-10); and *the stone tablets* on which God had inscribed the Ten Commandments, the ten chief covenant stipulations He required of Israel (see Exodus 31:18, 32:15-16).

Atonement cover (9:5). Read Exodus 25:17-22. The Hebrew word for "atonement" comes from the verb "to cover." When a sacrifice "atoned for" or "covered" a sin, the sin was paid for and so was covered from God's sight. Atonement is the act of divine grace by which God reconciles sinful people to Himself. In the Old Testament, the shed blood of a sacrifice atoned for sin; the animal paid the death penalty on the sinner's behalf (Leviticus 17:11).

The lid of the ark was called the "atonement cover" or "mercy seat" (KJV). Once each year, the high priest sacrificed a special sin offering and took its blood into the Most Holy Place where the ark stood. He would sprinkle the blood on the atonement cover to make atonement for the people's sins so that the tabernacle would stay holy and the Lord would remain among His people.

The atonement cover was also God's throne in the tabernacle (1 Samuel 4:4, 2 Samuel 6:2). A glowing cloud hovered above the cover as a visible manifestation of God's presence. The cloud was called God's *Glory*.

114

Flanking the Glory on either end of the atonement cover were two **cherubim**. These were carvings of angelic beings in the form of winged sphinxes. Such figures often adorned the armrests of royal thrones in the Near East. The cherubim flanked God's throne like royal attendants, their wings shielding the area where His presence was manifested.

For Further Study: How precise were the instructions for building the tabernacle (Exodus 36:8-38)? Why do you think God deemed this necessary?

1. From Hebrews 9:1-5 and the background in Exodus, what is your impression of the old covenant "regulations for worship" (9:1)? (For instance, what sense do you get of God? How complicated does the system seem? How does it seem different from the approach to worship you are used to?)

For Thought and Discussion: Why do you think God gave the earthly tabernacle and sacrificial system as an illustration or parable of Christ's once-for-all heavenly work?

_____

_____

_____

_____

_____

_____

_____

_____

Anticipating the new order (9:6-10)

Illustration (9:9). From this Greek word, *parabole*, we get our English word "parable." It means a symbol or object lesson. The whole earthly tabernacle was patterned on the heavenly dwelling of God as a picture to teach humans about that heavenly reality.

2. What do you think is the heavenly counterpart of each of the following?

115

For Further Study:
What does the lamp-
stand signify (see
Revelation 1:12-20)?

the Most Holy Place with the ark and the
atonement cover (see Hebrews 4:16, Revelation
4:1-5)

_____

_____

the golden cherubim (see Isaiah 6:1-3, Revelation 4:6-8)

_____

_____

_____

3. Read Leviticus 16:1-17. What do you learn
   about access to the Most Holy Place?

_____

_____

_____

4. What do you think this was meant to teach
   Israel? (See Hebrews 9:9-10.)

_____

_____

_____

_____

5. Why do you think the high priest had to bring a
   blood sacrifice when entering the Most Holy
   Place on the Day of Atonement (9:7)?

_____

_____

_____

_____

6. The way into the Most Holy Place was closed as long as the tabernacle or temple stood and the old covenant was in force (9:8). How did Jesus open the way into the Most Holy Place in heaven (10:19-20)?

_____

_____

_____

_____

_____

_____

7. How does Matthew 27:50-51 graphically illustrate this?

_____

_____

_____

_____

_____

New order (9:10). The new priesthood, the new heavenly sanctuary, and the new sacrifice—all part of the new covenant.

8. Why weren't the sacrifices of the old covenant "able to clear the conscience of the worshiper" (9:9)?

_____

_____

_____

_____

_____

For Thought and Discussion: a. How does "the conscience of the worshiper" (9:9) relate to his ability to "draw near to God" (7:19)? See also 4:16 and 10:22.
b. How is this affecting your life?

For Further Study: What does it mean that Christ is "the way" (John 10:9, 14:6; Ephesians 2:18, 3:12; Hebrews 9:8)?

For Further Study: On "the time of the new order" (Hebrews 9:10), think about Mark 1:15 and 2 Corinthians 5:17. What are the implications for you personally?

117

**Optional
Application:** a. Thank
God that your rela-
tionship to Him is not
based on "external
regulations" (9:10),
but on Christ's once-
for-all work.

b. Are you en-
snared in any external
regulations that are
hindering your fruitful
service to God? Pray
about this.

c. Are you carry-
ing around any guilt
and trying to atone for
it by work? If so, con-
fess it to God and let
Him cleanse your
conscience with
Jesus' blood.

9. How would you summarize the author's main point in 9:1-10?

_____

_____

_____

_____

Your response

10. What is the most significant truth you learned from studying 9:1-10 and its Old Testament background?

_____

_____

_____

_____

11. How is this truth relevant to your life?

_____

_____

_____

_____

_____

12. How can you act on what you have learned this week?

_____

_____

_____

_____

_____

13. List any questions you have about the material
in this lesson.

_____

_____

_____

_____

For the group

Warm-up. Ask, "Do you feel you have a clean conscience, or do feelings of guilt plague you?" If your
group is comfortable with each other, let members
answer aloud. If not, let everyone answer silently to
himself. When you discuss applications of 9:1-10,
emphasize that the point of Jesus' priestly work was
to clear your consciences. Guilt is your friend if it
drives you to confess, repent, and accept forgiveness. If anyone in your group feels unable to receive
God's forgiveness, plan time at the end of your
meeting to pray for that person, asking God to make
clear that Jesus has taken care of whatever sin it
may be.

Prayer. Thank God for illustrating Jesus' heavenly
work with the earthly tabernacle system. Thank Him
even more that Jesus has ushered in the new order,
in which your consciences can be utterly cleared of
guilt if you accept the forgiveness offered to you.

HEBREWS 9:11-28

A Superior Sacrifice

The whole elaborate tabernacle and sacrificial system of the Law was nothing but an illustration or parable to teach what blood sacrifice and atonement were all about (9:9). In 9:11-28, read about the reality the parable was pointing toward.

The blood of Christ (9:11-14)

Redemption (9:12). To obtain release (from slavery, prison, confiscation) by paying for the person or thing.

Ceremonially unclean (9:13). NASB: "defiled." A person who had become ceremonially unclean through contact with a corpse had to offer certain sacrifices in order to be cleansed (Numbers 19:1-22). The sacrificial system taught Israel that only shed blood could cleanse a person from the bloodguilt brought by sin, and only blood could cleanse a person from contamination by death so that he could approach the holy God. (See 9:22 and the box on page 128.)

Christ . . . Spirit . . . God (9:14). "With this lovely assertion, the writer of Hebrews involved all three Persons of the Godhead in the sacrifice of Christ, which magnifies the greatness of the redemptive offering."[1]

Acts that lead to death (9:14). Literally, "dead

For Thought and Discussion: What is "the greater and more perfect tabernacle" (9:11) that Christ entered? (See 9:24.)

Optional Application: Meditate on the fact that Christ's blood has cleansed you once for all "from acts that lead to death so that [you] may serve the living God" (9:14). How can you serve God out of gratitude for this cleansing this week? Take time to thank God for cleansing you.

121

works," probably a reference to the Levitical rituals. These were lifeless because they were incapable of imparting the life available in Christ.

1. What was cleansed under the old covenant (9:13)?

2. What is cleansed under the new covenant (9:14)?

3. What is the significance of "how much more" (9:14)?

Unblemished (9:14). The Law forbade Israel to offer blemished (wounded, blind, lame) animals for sacrifice (Deuteronomy 15:21, Malachi 1:8) because the animals' physical perfection had spiritual significance.

4. What did Christ make possible for believers by cleansing their consciences (9:14)?

_____

_____

_____

5. Summarize 9:11-14 in your own words.

_____

_____

_____

_____

_____

Christ the mediator (9:15)

Mediator (9:15). One who intervenes or intercedes between two persons, either to bring peace and friendship, to form a compact, or to ratify a covenant.

Ransom (9:15). NASB: "redemption." The price paid for release from bondage.

6. To what does "For this reason" (9:15) refer?

_____

_____

_____

_____

7. How does Christ act as the mediator of the new covenant?

_____

_____

For Further Study:
For more on our redemption, see Romans 3:24, 1 Corinthians 1:30, Galatians 3:13, Colossians 1:13-14, Titus 2:14, 1 Peter 1:18, and Revelation 5:9.

For Further Study:
On the ceremony described in Hebrews 9:19-21, see Exodus 24:6-8.

_____

_____

_____

8. Paraphrase 9:15 in your own words.

_____

_____

_____

_____

The necessity of shed blood (9:16-22)

Will (9:16). In this context, the word means "last will and testament," but it comes from the same word as "covenant."

9. The new covenant is like a will that bequeaths our "eternal inheritance" (9:15). What was necessary to bring this covenant or will into force (9:16-17)?

_____

_____

_____

10. Examine how Moses ratified the old covenant (9:18-21). How was the ratification of the new covenant like and unlike this?

like _____

_____

_____

unlike _____

_____

_____

124

11. Why was the shedding of blood necessary for forgiveness? (See Leviticus 17:11, and recall from pages 114 and 121 the meanings of atonement and redemption.)

_____

_____

_____

_____

_____

For Thought and Discussion: a. What are "the copies of the heavenly things" (9:23)?

b. What are "these sacrifices" (9:23)?

A better sacrifice (9:23-28)

12. How is the atonement, purification, or redemption wrought by Christ similar but superior to that under the old covenant system (9:22-28)?

similar _____

_____

_____

_____

_____

superior _____

_____

_____

_____

_____

13. Why do you think the author keeps emphasizing that Christ's sacrifice was "once for all" (9:12,26,28)?

_____

_____

For Thought and Discussion: What implications does the doctrine of judgment have for your daily lifestyle?

For Thought and Discussion: a. What did Christ accomplish at His first coming (9:26)?
 b. What will He accomplish at His second coming (9:28)?

For Thought and Discussion: How does modern man try to deal with his mortality? How should you (9:27-28)?

The end of the ages (9:26). The first coming of Christ (1 Peter 1:20). "His coming has ushered in the great messianic era, toward which all history has moved."[2]

Judgment (9:27). Both believers and unbelievers will be judged, but for different purposes. Believers are not judged in regard to the issue of salvation, but only in regard to rewards or loss of rewards (1 Corinthians 3:12-15, 2 Corinthians 5:10). Unbelievers, however, are headed for a judgment that leads to eternal punishment (Revelation 20:11-15).

Salvation (9:28). The full consummation of salvation when Christ ushers in the Kingdom in all its glory.

14. Why do you think the author looks ahead to Christ's return, bringing judgment and ultimate salvation? How is this relevant to the discussion at hand?

_____

_____

_____

_____

15. Summarize the basic message of 9:11-28.

_____

_____

_____

_____

126

Your response

16. What one truth from 9:11-28 seems most personally significant to you?

_____

_____

_____

_____

17. How would you like it to affect your life and attitudes?

_____

_____

_____

_____

18. What can you do to respond to this truth in a way that will begin letting it affect your life in concrete ways?

_____

_____

_____

_____

19. List any questions you have about 9:11-28.

_____

_____

_____

_____

_____

For Further Study: Add chapter 9 to your outline.

Optional Application: Does the fact of your mortality have any effect on the way you live? Explain.

For the group

Warm-up. Ask group members to think for a minute about blood sacrifice and being cleansed by blood.

127

These easily become spiritualized clichés and lose the shock God surely meant them to have. How is it possible that being drenched in someone's blood could make you clean? Don't talk about this now, just let the imagery sink in for a moment.

Questions. Don't try to cover all the questions in one meeting. Choose just those that seem most relevant to your group.

Prayer. Thank God that Christ's blood not only doesn't add to your guilt, but actually removes it utterly. Thank Him that His blood has really cleaned off all the other blood and dirt stains that have encrusted you. Praise Him that the price is paid, the work is finished, and you confidently await the salvation He will bring when He returns.

The Jewish Concept of Blood

The Jews believed that blood was sacred because the life of a creature is in its blood (Leviticus 17:11-14). Because blood was considered sacred, murder had to be punished with death, eating blood was forbidden, and the blood of an animal sacrifice could atone for a human's sin.

In Levitical worship, blood was used for three purposes: 1) the covenant between God and Israel was sealed by a blood rite; 2) blood was an essential element of sacrifices; and 3) blood was used in the consecration of priests.

The most important use of blood related to Hebrews is its use on the Day of Atonement. Leviticus 17:11 explains: "For the life of a creature is in the blood, and I have given it to you to make atonement for yourselves on the altar; it is the blood that makes atonement for one's life." The Jews accordingly believed: 1) the blood used for sacrifice was a divine provision; 2) shedding the blood of a sacrifice was a price-paying act; and 3) it was a substitutionary act. That is, the animals paid the death penalty as a substitute for the humans who deserved it. God established these principles of sacrifice to illustrate what Christ's ultimate sacrifice would accomplish.

---

1. Hodges, page 801.
2. *The NIV Study Bible*, page 1869.

HEBREWS 10:1-18

Once For All

Christ has superior priestly qualifications in the order of Melchizedek (7:1-28), and His superior ministry is based on a superior covenant (8:1-13). This was all made possible by His superior sacrifice (9:1-28). Now 10:1-18 wraps up this discussion of the priest and His sacrifice. Read the passage carefully.

The law a shadow (10:1-4)

Shadow (10:1). The Greek implies a pale shadow, not a sharp, distinct one.

Make perfect (10:1). Not sinless perfection, but "that definitive removal of guilt which makes free access to God possible."[1]

1. What are "the good things that are coming" of which the Law is a shadow (10:1)?

_____

_____

_____

_____

_____

For Further Study:
Compare "the good
things that are com-
ing" (10:1) to 9:11.
What is the point of
the contrast?

2. How do we know that the animal sacrifices were
   unable to make perfect those who worshiped
   under the old covenant (10:2)?

   _____

   _____

   _____

   _____

3. Contrast what the sacrificial system under the
   Law was not able to do (10:2) with what
   Christ's sacrifice was able to do (9:14).

   _____

   _____

   _____

   _____

   _____

4. What, then, was one purpose of the annual sacrifices (10:3)?

   _____

   _____

   _____

5. How was this beneficial?

   _____

   _____

   _____

   _____

The coming of Christ (10:5-10)

Hebrews 10:5-7 is quoted from Psalm 40:6-8, which expresses what Jesus said to His Father when He came into the world.

6. Because animal sacrifices did not please the Father, Jesus "[came] to do your will, O God" (Hebrews 10:7). What was the Father's will?

_____

_____

_____

_____

_____

7. Hebrews 10:5 says that the Father provided a body for Jesus. Why was it necessary for Him to have a body in order to accomplish His Father's will (10:10)?

_____

_____

_____

_____

_____

For Thought and Discussion: Why wasn't God pleased with sacrifices and offerings (10:6)?

For Thought and Discussion: a. How is Christ an example for all Christians in His affirmation to the Father: "Here I am, I have come to do your will" (10:9)?
   b. On this topic, see Psalms 40:8, 143:10; Matthew 12:50; Ephesians 6:6; James 4:15-17.

Sets aside (10:9). Annuls, just as a person's most recent legal will annuls all former ones.

One sacrifice (10:11-14)

Stands (10:11). "The Aaronic priests never sat down in the sanctuary; they remained standing throughout the whole performance of their sacred duties."² They never sat because their work was never done.

For Further Study:
Compare the phrase "the sacrifice of the body of Jesus Christ" (10:10) to Hebrews 2:14 and 1 Peter 2:24. Think about why it was necessary for Him to have a body.

For Further Study:
On Christ's enemies becoming His footstool, see Hebrews 1:13, Matthew 22:44, Psalm 110:1. What does this mean, and when will it happen?

8. Think about the treadmill routine of the Levitical priests (10:11). In contrast to this, what phrases in 10:12-14 emphasize the adequacy and finality of Christ's sacrifice?

10:12 _____

_____

_____

10:13 _____

_____

10:14 _____

_____

9. What does the sacrifice of Jesus' body accomplish for those who believe (10:10,14,16-17)?

_____

_____

_____

_____

_____

10. What does it mean that we *have been* "made perfect forever," yet "*are being* made holy" (10:14)?

_____

_____

_____

_____

_____

Forgiveness (10:15-18)

11. To summarize 10:1-18, look back at the absolute statements the author makes repeatedly, and complete the following in your own words.

132

a. the old covenant

"it can never" (10:1) _____

_____

_____

_____

"it is impossible" (10:4) _____

_____

_____

_____

b. the new covenant

"once for all" and "for all time" (10:10,12)

_____

_____

_____

"forever" (10:14) _____

_____

_____

_____

"no more" (10:17) _____

_____

12. How might these absolutes motivate believers
not to lapse back into the externals of Judaism?

_____

_____

_____

_____

_____

For Thought and Discussion: a. What contrast do you see between 10:1 and 10:14?
b. Contrast the blessings of the new covenant in 10:15-18 with the shortcomings of the old covenant (10:1-4).

For Thought and Discussion: Why is there no more sacrifice when sins are forgiven (10:18)?

Optional Application: What is your personal response to the fact that God has completely and irrevocably forgiven all of your sins?

133

Your response

13. What aspect of 10:1-18 would you like to take to heart this week?

_____

_____

_____

_____

_____

_____

14. What difference should this truth make to your life?

_____

_____

_____

_____

_____

15. How can you act on this truth this week?

_____

_____

_____

_____

16. List any questions you have about 10:1-18.

_____

_____

_____

_____

For the group

Warm-up. Ask everyone to think silently for a
moment about whether there is anything he or she
is having trouble *feeling* forgiven for today. Many
Christians, although fully aware of what Christ has
accomplished for them, still carry around a burden
of guilt. They are often scarcely aware of it, and they
may even try to ignore it because they know they
should act on facts rather than feelings. However,
buried feelings of guilt can affect our behavior in
many ways. Facing your feelings is the first step
toward letting go of them and choosing to act on
truth.

Questions. If guilt is a problem for anyone in your
group, explore all the reasons in 10:1-18 why you
know that Christ has dealt with your guilt. You
might also discuss why it is often so hard to believe
deep down that we are forgiven. How do the world,
the flesh, and the devil come into play here, and
how can you resist them?

Prayer. Thank Christ for obeying the Father and
offering Himself as the perfect sacrifice. Thank Him
that you have been made holy (set apart for God)
and are being made holy (gradually given the holy
character that goes along with your new status).
Thank Him especially that He has forgotten your
sins and lawless acts. Meditate together on 10:17,
and ask God to specifically forgive any of the sins
you have been carrying around.

1. Hodges, page 803.
2. Bruce, page 238.

HEBREWS 10:19-39

Perseverance

Now comes the climactic warning of the book. Having declared the ministry of Jesus as the supreme high priest, the author now forcefully points his readers to the implications of this truth. Read 10:19-39 at least twice.

A new and living way (10:19-25)

Confidence (10:19,35). The Greek word originally referred to the citizen's right to speak freely in democratic assemblies. It means "freedom to speak unreservedly" and "cheerful courage, boldness, and assurance."

1. What confidence do believers now have as a result of what Christ accomplished at the cross (10:19)? Explain in your own words.

_____

_____

_____

_____

2. Why does Jesus' blood give us this confidence?

_____

For Thought and Discussion: Where and how does the writer's mood change in **10:19-39?**

For Thought and Discussion: Which "Most Holy Place" do we have confidence to enter (**10:19**)—the heavenly or the earthly one? What are the implications of this?

137

For Thought and
Discussion: What
kept worshipers from
having the confidence
of 10:19 before Christ
came (9:9, 10:1-4)?

For Thought and
Discussion: "The
house of God" was a
Jewish expression for
the Temple. What
does the author mean
by "the house of God"
in 10:21? (See 3:6.)

New (10:20). Among the Greeks, this word originally meant "freshly slaughtered" or "newly
slain." Jesus is the new way, or the freshly
slaughtered sacrifice.

3. In view of what you know about the old covenant, how is it significant that Christ is a "living way" into the Most Holy Place (10:20)?

4. What does the author mean by calling Christ's
body "the curtain" (10:20)?

Therefore . . . since (10:19,21). These connecting
words indicate that these verses are the basis for
the exhortations in 10:22-25.

The Day approaching (10:25). Some scholars
believe this refers to the imminent destruction
of the Temple (just a few years after Hebrews
was written). Others think it may be a reference
to the Second Coming of Christ.

138

5. Verses 22-25 contain five important exhortations. List these.

Let us (10:22) ⸻

⸻

Let us (10:23) ⸻

⸻

Let us (10:24) ⸻

⸻

Let us (10:25) ⸻

⸻

Let us (10:25) ⸻

⸻

6. The triad of faith, hope, and love is mentioned over and over in Scripture. How does the author use this triad to address the needs of his readers under persecution?

faith (10:22) ⸻

⸻

⸻

⸻

hope (10:23) ⸻

⸻

⸻

⸻

love (10:24) ⸻

⸻

⸻

⸻

For Thought and Discussion: a. How should we relate to God, according to 10:22-23?

b. How should we relate to fellow Christians (10:24-25)?

Optional Application: a. Take a brief spiritual inventory of your life based on 10:22-25. Prayerfully consider how well you are . . .

drawing near to God with a sincere heart in full assurance of faith (10:22).

holding unswerving to the hope you profess (10:23).

spurring others on toward love and good deeds (10:24).

meeting together with other Christians (10:25).

encouraging others (10:25).

b. What commitments does this self-examination move you to make? Pray about this also.

7. Why do you think these persecuted Christians were tempted to "give up meeting together" (10:25)?

_____

_____

_____

_____

_____

8. Why should "the Day approaching" motivate believers to meet together and encourage each other?

_____

_____

_____

_____

_____

A sober warning (10:26-31)

Knowledge (10:26). The Greek word denotes full, complete knowledge and understanding.

9. In the context of 10:19-39, what sin do you think the author is talking about in 10:26? (Or do you think he means sin in general?) Why?

_____

_____

_____

_____

_____

10. If the Hebrew Christians reject Christ's provision for sin, what can they expect (10:26-27)?

_____

_____

_____

_____

_____

11. Why should they expect this (10:28-29)?

_____

_____

_____

_____

_____

_____

Optional Application: How can you take to heart the warning to avoid the sin in 10:26,35,39?

For Thought and Discussion: How can a modern Christian "trample" the Son of God?

Trampled (10:29). Scorned or counted as worthless. This is the attitude of one who, while walking on the sidewalk, sees a penny on the ground and walks by it or kicks it into the gutter. The penny is considered worthless and so is trampled.

---

12. What aspects of God's character should motivate us to think twice before disregarding Christ (10:30-31)?

_____

_____

_____

_____

_____

For Further Study:
On divine vengeance, see Deuteronomy 32:35, Psalm 94:1, Ezekiel 25:17, Micah 5:15, Nahum 1:2, Romans 12:19. How do you relate this aspect of God to His holiness? How do you relate it to His love?

For Further Study:
a. What do you learn from 11:10, 13-16,26,35; 13:14 about the "better and lasting possessions" (10:34)?
  b. How would these possessions motivate believers to remain faithful in the midst of severe persecution?

13. Summarize . . .

    the exhortation (10:19-25) _____

    _____

    _____

    _____

    the warning (10:26-31) _____

    _____

    _____

    _____

Better and lasting possessions
(10:32-39)

Remember (10:32). Carefully think back, reconstruct in the mind. The present tense in Greek means that this should be a continuous action or habit.

Publicly exposed (10:33). From the Greek word *theatrizo*, from which we get our word "theater." It refers to bringing upon the stage or setting forth as a spectacle.

14. What does 10:32-33 reveal about the previous experiences of this group of Hebrew Christians?

    _____

    _____

    _____

    _____

    _____

15. How did they respond (10:34)?

    _____

    _____

16. Why did they respond this way (10:34)?

17. Why do you think the author exhorts them to remember these early days?

Optional Application: How are you being tempted to "shrink back" (10:39)? How can you go about resisting this temptation?

For Thought and Discussion: What kind of "confidence" is the author referring to in 10:35? (Recall 10:19.)

For Thought and Discussion: How does the author use prophecy as a motivation in 10:37?

18. With what "better and lasting possessions" (10:34) will we be "richly rewarded" (10:35) as God "has promised" (10:36) if we persevere in confidence and doing God's will?

19. What does it mean to "shrink back" (10:39)?

Optional Application: Does your future reward (10:35) and promised inheritance (10:36) help you persevere in times of stress? What have you learned in this lesson that might help you in this regard? Meditate on these truths, and remind yourself of them when under pressure.

For Further Study: Add 10:19-39 to your outline.

20. Summarize the main message of 10:19-39.

_____

_____

_____

_____

_____

_____

Your response

21. What one exhortation or promise from 10:19-39 would you like to take to heart this week?

_____

_____

_____

_____

_____

22. How would you like it to affect your life?

_____

_____

_____

_____

23. What steps can you take to act on this?

_____

_____

_____

_____

24. List any questions you have about 10:19-39.

_____

_____

_____

_____

For the group

Warm-up. Ask, "Describe the last time someone encouraged you to persevere in faith. What did he or she do that encouraged you?"

Questions. This is an unusually long lesson. You might want to plan two meetings to cover it.

Hebrews 10:26-31 has troubled many Christians because of its severity. Give each member of your group a chance to voice any concerns about the passage. Try to deal with any questions raised.

How can you "spur one another on toward love and good deeds" (10:24)?

Prayer. Draw near to God in full assurance of faith, thanking Him for the new and living way opened for you by Jesus. Thank God for the hope and inheritance before you, and ask Him to strengthen each of you to persevere in active faith. Pray for any group members suffering persecution.

The Siege of Jerusalem

Judea had been seething for decades; even in the time of Jesus, the Zealots were fomenting rebellion and the Romans were poised to crush any attempts. In 68 AD, the resistance finally erupted into war.

After quelling the countryside, general Titus and his soldiers began the siege of Jerusalem in April of 70 AD. Efforts to persuade the Jewish population of the city to surrender, and thus preserve the city, had failed. So Titus encircled the city with an impenetrable wall of soldiers to prevent any help from reaching those within, and launched his final attack.

(continued on page 146)

(continued from page 145)
First the outer cloisters of the Temple were burned, and finally—five months after the siege began—the inner court of the Temple was surrounded. In the attack the following day, a Roman soldier tossed a firebrand through a window into one of the side chambers, while another soldier threw a burning brand into the Holy Place. The entire sanctuary burst into flames.

During the battle, some of the priests on the roof pulled up spikes used to keep birds off the building and hurled them unavailingly at the relentless Romans. Eventually, the entire temple complex was engulfed in fire. Last of all fell the Royal Portico, where about six thousand people who had sought refuge perished. The Jewish sacrificial system was no more.

HEBREWS 11:1-40

By Faith

"But my righteous one will live by faith," the author quotes in 10:38. Yet, what is faith that is pleasing to God? Is it simply an intellectual assent that Jesus is the Christ, an assent that leaves one free to live outwardly indistinguishable from the world around one? Can a Hebrew Christian have faith and still conform to Jewish ritual? Can a Gentile Christian have faith and live like a pagan?

In chapter 11, the author describes vividly the kind of faith he has in mind. Read the whole chapter carefully.

For Further Study: Compare Hebrews 11:1-2 to 2 Corinthians 4:16-18. What additional insights do you gain about living by faith?

Being sure (11:1). This Greek word was widely used in legal circles of a person's "evidence of ownership" of either property or land. Hence, the sense in 11:1 is, "Faith is the title-deed of what we hope for."

1. What are the key elements of faith (11:1)?

_____

_____

_____

_____

_____

For Thought and Discussion: What is the basis for a Christian's faith that God created the universe?

For Thought and Discussion: How does Abel "still speak, even though he is dead" (Hebrews 11:4)? See Genesis 4:10, Hebrews 12:24.

For Further Study: Read about Enoch in Genesis 5:18-24.

For Further Study: How can believers please God (Hebrews 11:5)? See Matthew 3:17, John 8:29, Hebrews 13:16.

2. How does 11:2 set the theme for the rest of the chapter?

_____

_____

_____

_____

_____

3. How is belief that the universe was created by God (11:3) a good example of the kind of faith defined in 11:1?

_____

_____

_____

_____

_____

_____

4. How is Abel (11:4) an example of faith as defined in 11:1? (*Optional:* See Genesis 4:1-4.)

_____

_____

_____

_____

_____

5. According to Hebrews 11:6, there are two requirements that must be satisfied by those who come to God. List these.

a. _____

_____

b. _____

_____

6. Why are both of these necessary?

_____

_____

_____

_____

_____

_____

Holy fear (11:7). Pious care or concern. A genuine spiritual devotion and a great respect for the things of God.

_____

7. Since Noah lived in a dry area about five hundred miles from the sea, how did building the ark demonstrate his faith in God (11:1,7)?

_____

_____

_____

_____

_____

_____

For Thought and Discussion: a. How did Noah's "holy fear" of God relate to his faith (11:7)?
b. How do you think Noah's faith "condemned the world" (11:7)?
c. What was Noah's reward (11:7)?

For Further Study: On "holy fear" see Nehemiah 5:15-16; Job 1:1-5,21-22; Acts 5:1-11; 10:2. How can you show this kind of holy fear that leads to active faith?

City with foundations (11:10). The heavenly and eternal Jerusalem (Hebrews 12:22, 13:14; Revelation 21:1-22:6).

Sarah (11:11). As the NIV text note explains, there are textual variants that make it uncertain whether this verse is about Abraham's or Sarah's faith. Compare several versions.

As good as dead (11:12). Abraham was one hundred years old (Genesis 21:5, Romans 4:19).

149

For Further Study:
What insights do you gain from Genesis 47:9; Exodus 6:4; 1 Chronicles 29:15; Psalms 39:12, 119:19; Philippians 3:20; 1 Peter 2:11 regarding the idea that believers are "aliens and strangers on the earth" (Hebrews 11:13)?

Optional Application: Do you consider yourself a pilgrim and an alien on the earth? How does this affect your priorities and actions? How should it affect them in deeper ways?

8. How did Abraham demonstrate his faith (11:8-10)?

_____

_____

_____

_____

_____

9. How were Abraham and Sarah rewarded for their faith (11:11-12)?

_____

_____

_____

_____

10. Why did Abraham feel confident in placing his faith in God (11:11)?

_____

_____

_____

_____

_____

Did not receive (11:13). Neither Abraham, Isaac, nor Jacob ever possessed the promised land. Israel did not begin to take possession until almost five hundred years after Jacob died. Verse 13 applies to Abel, Enoch, and Noah as well.

11. Why did all these people hang onto their faith, even though they never saw what they hoped for during their earthly lives (11:13-16)?

_____

_____

_____

_____

_____

12. How were Abraham's actions in Genesis 22:1-18 (Hebrews 11:17-19) an example of the faith defined in Hebrews 11:1?

_____

_____

_____

_____

13. How did the actions of Isaac, Jacob, and Joseph (the successive heirs of the promises to Abraham) demonstrate faith (11:20-22)?

_____

_____

_____

_____

_____

_____

For Thought and Discussion: How would 11:13-16 minister to Hebrew believers suffering terrible persecution?

For Further Study: On Hebrews 11:20-22, see Genesis 27:27-40, 47:29-31, 48:8-20, 50:24-25.

For Thought and Discussion: List the acts of faith you find in 11:23-29.

For Thought and Discussion: How did faith enable Moses to see "him who is invisible" (Hebrews 11:1,6,27)?

King's edict (11:23). Pharaoh had ordered that all male Hebrew babies be killed at birth (Exodus 1:22-2:4). **Pharaoh's daughter** (11:24) adopted the infant Moses (Exodus 2:5-10).

For the sake of Christ (11:26). At the time, God had revealed only the dimmest outline of the hope that would one day be fulfilled by Christ, but Moses chose to be identified with the people of the promise anyway.

151

For Further Study:
For the full story of
Jericho and Rahab,
see Joshua 2:1-24,
6:1-27. How did
Rahab and Israel
show faith in that
situation? What was
Rahab risking when
she chose to put her
faith in the God of
Israel rather than in
her own people?

For Further Study:
The Old Testament
faithful were all ordi-
nary human beings
with failures and
shortcomings like
anyone else. (See, for
instance, Genesis
12:10-13, Exodus
2:14, Joshua 7:6-9.)
What does this reveal
about what faith can
accomplish even
through imperfect
people?

Persevered (11:27). After fleeing Egypt for Midian
(Exodus 2:11-15), Moses spent forty years keep-
ing sheep in Midian, then returned to Egypt at
God's command to face Pharaoh.

Passover and sprinkling (11:28). To prove His
supremacy and force Pharaoh to release Israel,
God struck dead every firstborn human and
animal in Egypt. However, He told the Israelites
to protect themselves from this plague by sprinkling the blood of a sacrificed lamb on the door-
frames of their houses. He told them to feast on
the sacrificed lambs as a celebration of His
redemption; the feast was called the Passover
because it marked the day when the angel of
death passed over the Israelites but struck the
Egyptians (Exodus 12:1-51).

Walls of Jericho (11:30). Many city walls of that
period were so wide at the top that two chariots
could drive side by side. Jericho was a frontier
fortress, and its walls were designed to with-
stand the attack of even the strongest enemies.
By the standards of the day, it was considered
impregnable.

Tortured (11:35). From the Greek word *tympanizo*,
from which we get our word *tympany*, or kettle-
drum. This type of torture involved stretching
the victim over a large drum-like apparatus and
beating him with clubs, often until dead.

14. How did Moses show faith (11:23-28)?

_____

_____

_____

_____

_____

_____

_____

15. Read how the people described in 11:32-38 showed faith. Why were their faith and suffering worthwhile, even though they never received what was promised (11:39-40)?

_____

_____

_____

_____

_____

16. In what sense could the Old Testament saints "be made perfect" only together with New Testament believers (11:40)?

_____

_____

_____

_____

_____

17. Review chapter 11, this time paying special attention to the *requirements of faith*. What can you sift from the following verses about what is required for faith to be effective?

11:6 _____

_____

_____

11:8 _____

_____

11:11 _____

_____

For Further Study:
Study the background of Gideon (Judges 6:11, 8:32), Barak (Judges 4:6-5:31), Samson (Judges 13:24-16:31), Jephthah (Judges 11:1-12:7), David (1 Samuel 16:1-17:58), Samuel (1 Samuel 7:1-10:8, 12:1-13:15), shutting the mouths of lions (Judges 14:5, 1 Samuel 17:34, Daniel 6:1-28), quenching fire (Daniel 3:1-28), and a woman receiving her dead back (1 Kings 17:22-23, 2 Kings 4:35-36).

Optional Application: Is there a particular biblical character mentioned in chapter 11 with whom you identify and to whom you can look as a model for living by faith? If so, who is it, and how is that person a model for you in your situation? How can you follow that model?

Optional Application: a. Does exercising faith always involve some measure of not knowing (11:8)? Why or why not?
b. Is there any circumstance in your life in which you need to trust God, even though you can't see where it is all going to lead? What have you learned from chapter 11 that makes it easier for you to do this?

11:27 _____

_____

_____

18. How does this chapter on faith contribute to the author's overall purpose of convincing his Hebrew readers not to lapse away from Christianity when under pressure?

_____

_____

_____

_____

_____

_____

Your response

19. What have you learned from 11:1-40 about faith that is especially relevant to your current situation?

_____

_____

_____

_____

_____

20. How does your current situation call for this kind of faith? How can you act in faith this week under these circumstances?

_____

_____

_____

154

_____

_____

_____

_____

_____

21. List any questions you have about 11:1-40.

_____

_____

_____

_____

For the group

Warm-up. Ask each person to name one thing he or she is hoping for from God that He has promised but has not yet fulfilled. This can be a promise specific to the person, or a biblical promise that the person holds especially dear.

Questions. Allow about half of your time to examine how the author defines faith in chapter 11 and how the people described in the chapter reflect that kind of faith. Then allow the other half of your time to share the situations you are each facing that call for this kind of faith. Discuss how each of you can show the kind of faith that is certain about what you don't see because you know that He who has promised is faithful and rewards those who seek and obey Him, the kind of faith that focuses on Him who is invisible and on the heavenly city that awaits you. What acts of trusting obedience is God asking of each of you? Be open about the circumstances you are facing.

Prayer. Praise God that He is faithful to fulfill His promises. Ask Him to help each of you trust Him who is invisible and act in faith that He will do what He has promised for you.

HEBREWS 12:1-29

Discipline and Commitment

From Abel to Zechariah, the Old Testament saints testified to their faith in hardship, persecution, and death (11:1-40). How should this "cloud of witnesses" affect what we do now? Read 12:1-29, looking for the overall point of the chapter.

For Further Study: Some examples of things that hinder can be found in Matthew 19:21-22; Luke 9:57-62, 12:27-31.

Run the race (12:1-4)

Cloud of witnesses (12:1). A witness is literally one who testifies to what he has seen or heard or knows. The phrase, "cloud of witnesses," is used not in the sense of "spectators watching their successors as they in turn run the race, but rather in the sense that by their loyalty and endurance they have borne witness to the possibilities of the life of faith."[1]

Everything that hinders (12:1). The phrase literally refers to a bulk or mass of something that is not necessarily bad in itself. It may be something that is perfectly innocent and harmless, but it weighs one down and diverts one's attention away from where it should be.

The sin (12:1). The use of the definite article (*the* sin) seems to indicate that the author had a specific sin in mind. It was probably the sin of lapsing away from Christianity in unbelief and unfruitfulness.

**Optional
Application:** a. How
well would you say
you are running the
Christian race
(12:1-2)? Are you
persevering? Fixing
your eyes on Jesus?
Following Jesus'
example in letting
your future glory and
joy be a motivation
for endurance?
   b. If your running
is not up to par, what
do you find in chapter
12 that might help
you? What steps can
you take this week to
run with perseverance
and fix your eyes on
Jesus?

1. "Since we are surrounded by such a great cloud
   of witnesses" (12:1), what two exhortations
   does the author give us?

   a. _____

   _____

   _____

   b. _____

   _____

   _____

2. What are some of the things that might be
   included in "everything that hinders" (12:1)?

   _____

   _____

   _____

   _____

   _____

Endured the cross (12:2). "To die by crucifixion was
   to plumb the lowest depths of disgrace; it was a
   punishment reserved for those who were
   deemed of all men most unfit to live, a punishment for sub-men. From so degrading a death
   Roman citizens were exempt by ancient statute;
   the dignity of the Roman name would be be-
   smirched by being brought into association
   with anything so vile as the cross. For slaves,
   and criminals of low degree, it was regarded as a
   suitable means of execution, and a grim deter-
   rent to others."[2]

3. What should be our inspiration in running the
   race with perseverance (12:2-3)?

   _____

   _____

_____

_____

_____

4. Practically speaking, what do you think it means to "fix our eyes" on Jesus (12:2)?

_____

_____

_____

_____

For Thought and Discussion: What does the phrase, "the author and perfecter of our faith" (12:2) mean?

Optional Application: What tempts you to "grow weary and lose heart" (12:3)? How can fixing your eyes on Jesus help you resist this temptation?

5. Jesus' motivation for enduring the cross and its shame was "the joy set before him" (12:2). What joy is set before you that can motivate you to endure and persevere? (*Optional:* See Romans 8:18-23, 2 Corinthians 4:17, Philippians 3:20-21.)

_____

_____

_____

_____

_____

God disciplines His children (12:5-11)

Discipline (12:5). The ancient Greeks used this word to refer to the training of a child. It signified whatever parents and teachers did to train, correct, cultivate, and educate children in order to help them mature properly.

Punishes (12:6). NASB: "scourges." This word was used for flogging with a whip, a practice common among the Jews. It referred to a severe and extremely painful beating. It indicates that God's discipline can sometimes be severe, espe-

159

**Optional
Application:** What
state might your life
be in today if God
chose not to disci-
pline you when you
went astray? Take a
few minutes to thank
Him for His love as
demonstrated in His
corrective discipline
in your life.

For Further Study:
What different forms
does God's discipline
take in the life of a
believer (Psalms
32:3-5; 38:1-8;
39:1-13;
119:67,71,75;
1 Corinthians
11:27-32; 2 Corinthi-
ans 12:7-10)?

**Optional
Application:** Has
God's discipline pro-
duced a harvest of
righteousness and
peace in your life? If
not, is there some-
thing in your life that
is causing you to be
stubborn or hard-
hearted in your rela-
tionship to God? What
in chapter 12 might
help you correct any
wrong attitudes you
have regarding God's
discipline?

cially when a believer's disobedience or apathy
is blatant and continuous.

Endure hardship (12:7). These Hebrew Christians
were experiencing ridicule, economic discrimi-
nation, and even violence from nonChristian
Jews—*opposition from sinful men* (12:3) like
Jesus suffered.

6. Why shouldn't we lose heart when the Lord
rebukes or disciplines us (12:5-9)?

_____

_____

_____

_____

_____

_____

Father of our spirits (12:9). In contrast to our individual "fathers of the flesh."

7. For what purposes does the Father chasten
believers? What does discipline produce in the
life of a believer (12:10-11)?

_____

_____

_____

_____

Spiritual commitment (12:12-17)

8. Practically speaking, what would be involved in
putting the exhortations of 12:12-13 into
practice?

_____

_____

_____

_____

_____

_____

_____

For Thought and Discussion: Why do you think it is impossible for an unholy person to see the Lord (12:14)?

For Further Study: On living in peace with all men, see Mark 9:50; Romans 12:18, 14:19. Why is it important to live at peace with *all* men, including unbelievers?

Make every effort (12:14). In its literal sense, the phrase means "to run swiftly in order to catch someone or something." Used metaphorically, it means "eagerly pursue," or "earnestly endeavor to acquire."

For Thought and Discussion: How were some of these Hebrew believers in danger of missing "the grace of God" (12:15)? Review 2:1-4, 6:4-8.

9. In a situation where some of the believers were lapsing away from active faith, others were struggling to hold on, and all were under pressure from neighbors and coworkers, why would an exhortation to "live in peace with all men" (12:14) be appropriate?

_____

_____

_____

_____

_____

_____

Bitter root (12:15). In Deuteronomy 29:18, Moses uses this expression to describe rebelliousness in the heart that produces the poison of idolatry. Other bitter roots that defile a group are pride, animosity, and rivalry.

Esau (12:16). See Genesis 25:29-34.

Optional Application: Are there any bitter roots in your heart defiling you and others? If so, confess them to God, and ask Him to forgive you and cleanse you with the blood of Christ. If the bitter root is unforgiveness of someone else, forgive that person. Commit yourself to act as Jesus would in that situation.

Optional Application: Are you experiencing Esau's temptation? If so, what can you do about it?

10. How were the Hebrew recipients of this letter tempted to be like Esau (Hebrews 12:16-17)?

_____

_____

_____

_____

_____

_____

_____

A final warning (12:18-28)

Mountain (12:18). The old covenant was given on Mt. Sinai in an awesome manifestation of God's holiness (Exodus 19:10-25). The author of Hebrews refers to this event again when he speaks of *him who warned them on earth* (12:25) and *his voice shook the earth* (12:26).

Church of the firstborn (12:23). Believers in general. "Firstborn" is plural, and *whose names are written in heaven* generally refers to the redeemed (Revelation 3:5, 13:8, 17:8, 20:12, 21:27). They are the firstborn in that they are heirs together with Christ, the supreme firstborn.

Spirits of righteous men made perfect (12:23). "They are surely believers of pre-Christian days, like those mentioned in Ch. 11:40, who could not be 'made perfect' until Christ came in the fulness of time and 'by one offering . . . perfected for ever them that are sanctified.'"[3]

11. Contrast what the author says about the old covenant (12:18-21) and the new (12:22-24). What are the primary differences?

old	new

For Thought and Discussion: Why would 12:18-24 tend to discourage a Hebrew believer from lapsing from the new covenant system back into the old covenant system?

For Thought and Discussion: a. What "word" did Abel's blood speak (12:24)? See Genesis 4:10.
b. What "better word" does the blood of Jesus speak (9:12, 10:19)?

12. In view of the wonders and privileges of the new covenant, what warning does the author give his readers (12:25)?

_____

_____

_____

_____

Once more I will shake . . . (12:26). A quotation from Haggai 2:6, which refers to God's future judgment of the nations when Christ returns.

13. After this future shaking occurs, what will remain? What is it that "cannot be shaken" (12:27-28)?

_____

_____

_____

_____

163

For Further Study:
On worshiping God
acceptably, see
1 Chronicles 16:29;
Psalms 95:6, 96:9;
Matthew 4:10; John
4:19-24; Romans
12:1; Revelation
14:7, 15:4. Based on
these verses, how
would you define
worship?

For Further Study:
Add chapter 12 to
your outline.

14. How should we respond to this assurance (12:28)?

_____

_____

_____

_____

_____

15. Why do you think the author brings this section to a close with the quotation from Deuteronomy 4:24, "For our 'God is a consuming fire'" (12:29)?

_____

_____

_____

_____

_____

16. Summarize 12:1-29 in your own words.

_____

_____

_____

_____

Your response

17. What one truth from chapter 12 seems most personally significant to you today?

_____

164

_____

_____

_____

_____

18. How would you like this truth to affect your life in a deeper way?

_____

_____

_____

_____

19. What can you do to act on this truth this week?

_____

_____

_____

_____

20. List any questions you have about 12:1-29.

_____

_____

_____

_____

For the group

Warm-up. Ask, "How have you experienced God's discipline during the past week?"

165

Prayer. Thank God for the cloud of witnesses testifying to the rewards of faith, for the example of Jesus' endurance, for the discipline that produces the harvest of righteousness and peace, and for the promise of the heavenly Jerusalem. Ask Him to help each of you endure in your circumstances. Take some time to worship God with reverence and awe.

1. Bruce, page 346.
2. Bruce, page 352.
3. Bruce, page 378.

HEBREWS 13:1-25

Exhortations

"Therefore . . . let us run with perseverance the race marked out for us" (12:1). "Therefore . . . let us be thankful, and so worship God acceptably" (12:28). What are some practical ways for a group of persecuted believers to run and worship? Read 13:1-25.

For Further Study:
On entertaining angels, see Genesis 18; Judges 6, 13.

Entertain (13:2). Well-built and relatively well-policed roads had made civilian travel possible in the Roman Empire as it had never been before. One of the chief reasons why the gospel spread so rapidly was that missionaries, businesspeople, and tourists could walk or ride from Syria to Spain. However, there were few inns along the roads, and they were dirty, thief-infested, and expensive. Since military and government officials had the right to commandeer lodgings from people who lived along the roads, fed-up villagers often turned away ordinary travelers. Therefore, hospitality was considered an obligation of brotherhood among Christians.

1. Verses 2 and 3 give examples of verse 1. Why is each of the following an important manifestation of genuine love?

entertaining strangers _____

167

For Further Study:
a. What do you learn
about brotherly love
(Hebrews 13:1) from
John 13:34-35 and
1 John 3:14-17?
  b. What do you
learn from Job 31:32;
Matthew 25:34-35,
37-40; and 1 Peter
4:9 about showing
hospitality?
  c. What do Mat-
thew 25:36-40 and
Colossians 4:18 have
to say about remem-
bering those in
prison?

**For Thought and
Discussion:** How are
the admonitions in
13:1-3 particularly
relevant to these
Hebrew believers?

remembering those in prison _____

_____

_____

_____

_____

Pure (13:4). Free from contamination.

2. The author has stressed throwing off hindrances, living at peace, and being holy
   (12:1,14). What two examples of holiness and
   avoiding hindrances does he single out for mention in 13:4-5?

   13:4 _____

   _____

   13:5 _____

   _____

3. Why is it so important to honor marriage and
   keep the marriage bed pure (13:4)? (*Optional:*
   See 1 Corinthians 6:12-20, Ephesians 5:25-32.)

   _____

   _____

   _____

   _____

4. a. What fears does the author imply often lie at
      the root of the love of money (13:5-6)?

168

b. How does he try to disperse these fears?

_____

_____

_____

_____

_____

_____

Optional Application: Do you have trouble being peacefully content with your level of income and possessions? Do you have a settled confidence that the Lord will always be there to protect you from financial disaster if you are walking obediently with Him? Examine your financial attitudes and practices in light of 13:5-6. Do you need to make any changes?

The love of money (13:5). The Jewish high priest in Jerusalem had the authority to throw defecting Jews into jail. It was a serious financial disaster for a family when the head of the house was jailed. Furthermore, those defectors who escaped imprisonment often lost their jobs. Accordingly, the temptation to love money and not trust God to provide was great.

Consider (13:7). To look upon a subject in order to investigate and observe it accurately.

Leaders who spoke the word of God to you (13:7). Probably apostles (2:3). These Hebrew Christians had first heard the gospel some years ago (5:12), and 13:7 implies that the outcome of their leaders' lives is now apparent because those leaders are now dead.[1]

For Further Study: On material wealth and contentment, see Luke 12:15-21, Philippians 4:10-13, and 1 Timothy 6:6-10. Why does Scripture address the issue of money so often?

5. What three exhortations does the author give regarding these former leaders (13:7)?

_____

_____

_____

For Further Study:
On imitating godly
leaders, see Hebrews
6:12; 1 Corinthians
4:16; 1 Thessaloni-
ans 1:6-7, 2:14;
3 John 11. Do you
know any Christian
leader who is worthy
of such imitation?

6. How does the assertion in 13:8 relate to 13:7?

_____

_____

_____

_____

_____

Carried away (13:9). The Greek present tense gives
the idea of "stop being carried away." Not only
was the danger present, but some were already
in the process of being carried away.

7. Read 13:9-10. In this context, what are the
"strange doctrines" of 13:9?

_____

_____

_____

_____

8. At what altar—from what sacrifice—do Christians alone have the right to eat (13:10)?
(*Optional:* See 1 Corinthians 5:7-8.)

_____

_____

_____

_____

170

Burned outside the camp (13:11). Under the Levitical system, a sin offering was burned outside
the camp or city, away from the Holy Place,
because it carried the defilement of the people's
sin (Leviticus 4:12, 16:27-28). This was especially true of the sin offering on the Day of
Atonement.
  Jesus was executed outside the gates of
Jerusalem, at Golgotha (Mark 15:20-22).

9. What does the fact that Jesus was killed outside
Jerusalem tell us about Him (Hebrews
13:11-12)?

_____

_____

_____

_____

10. What does "Let us, then, go to Him outside the
camp" mean (13:13)?

_____

_____

_____

_____

_____

11. Why should Christians do this (13:14)?

_____

_____

_____

_____

For Thought and Discussion: Does 13:17 imply slavish obedience to dictatorial leaders? What is the witness of the rest of Scripture on this subject?

Optional Application: Do you try to make your leaders' work joyful and not burdensome? How can you do this better?

For Thought and Discussion:
a. What picture is given of God in the benediction of 13:20-21?
  b. What picture is given of Jesus?
  c. How is this benediction an appropriate conclusion to the book in view of the book's purpose?

12. As opposed to animal sacrifices offered under the old covenant, what two sacrifices are Christians now to offer God?

13:15 _____

_____

13:16 _____

_____

13. What should motivate us to obey and submit to our leaders (13:17)?

_____

_____

_____

_____

_____

Leaders (13:17). Their present leaders, as opposed to the former ones mentioned in 13:7.

14. How does the benediction (blessing) in 13:20-21 summarize some of the main emphases in the book of Hebrews?

_____

_____

_____

_____

_____

15. Summarize 13:1-25 in your own words.

_____

_____

_____

_____

_____

Your response

16. What one aspect of chapter 13 would you like to take to heart this week?

_____

_____

_____

_____

_____

17. What action can you take in response to this?

_____

_____

_____

_____

_____

_____

18. List any questions you have about 13:1-25.

_____

_____

_____

_____

For Further Study: Add 13:1-25 to your outline.

Optional Application: Prayerfully evaluate your current life in the following areas. Ask God to make clear where you are fruitful and where you are falling short:
hospitality
remembering those in prison
purity in marriage
proper attitude on material wealth
appreciation for grace
offering praise to God
doing good and sharing with others
obedience to leaders
prayer.
If you feel that you are below God's desires for you in any of these areas, what action can you take?

For the group

Warm-up. Ask each person to share one opportunity he or she has had during the past week to run the

Optional Application: Pray 13:20-21 for yourself and others.

race with perseverance. Describe briefly how your efforts to persevere have been going.

Prayer. Take time to offer a sacrifice of praise to the God of peace and the Lord who offered Himself outside the camp as a sin offering for you. Ask God to help each of you love in the ways described in chapter 13. You might use 13:20-21 as a model for prayer for each other, perhaps pairing off to pray specifically for one other person.

Material Wealth

Under the old covenant, God promised to bless His people if they obeyed Him (Deuteronomy 28:1-14). Some Jewish leaders, through a perversion of this principle, taught that material possessions were a sure sign of God's favor. Their view is summed up in the saying, "Whom the Lord loves He makes rich." Conversely, these teachers believed that poverty was a sign of God's disfavor. They accordingly sought money and possessions in order to prove that they were accepted and approved by God. Jesus decried this view, emphasizing God's love for those with a poor man's humility and dependence on God, and New Testament writers followed Him in warning frequently against the love of money.

1. *The NIV Study Bible*, page 1876.

REVIEW

Looking Back

After studying a book in detail for several weeks, it is often helpful to pull together what you have learned and examine the book as a whole again. A review can enable you to see how each individual topic the author talks about contributes to the overall point he wants to make. It can also help you trace themes and related ideas from chapter to chapter.

This review is fairly thorough. Feel free to take extra time to complete it or to omit some sections.

1. First, reread all of Hebrews. It should be familiar by now, so you should be able to read rapidly, looking for threads that tie the book together. Pray for a fresh perspective on what God is saying.

2. What has Hebrews taught you about how Christ is superior to . . .

   Old Testament prophets? _____

   _____

   _____

   _____

   _____

   _____

   _____

angels? _____

_____

_____

_____

_____

_____

_____

Moses? _____

_____

_____

_____

_____

_____

_____

the Aaronic high priests? _____

_____

_____

_____

_____

_____

_____

the sacrifices those priests offered? _____

_____

_____

_____

_____

_____

_____

_____

3. What have you learned from Hebrews about . . .

proof that Jesus is God? _____

_____

_____

_____

_____

_____

_____

_____

spiritual maturity? _____

_____

_____

_____

_____

_____

For Thought and Discussion: What have you learned from Hebrews about . . .
the superiority of the new covenant over the old?
the earthly tabernacle versus the heavenly one?
God's discipline of His children?
future glory as a motivation for living?
brotherly love?

unbelief and lapsing away from Christ? _____

_____

_____

_____

_____

_____

_____

entering God's rest? _____

_____

_____

_____

_____

perseverance and endurance? _____

_____

_____

_____

_____

_____

_____

faith? _____

_____

_____

_____

_____

_____

_____

_____

4. How would you summarize the main message of Hebrews?

_____

_____

_____

_____

_____

_____

_____

5. Review the questions you listed at the ends of lessons one through eighteen. Do any important ones remain unanswered? If so, some of the sources on pages 181-185 may help you answer some of them. You might also study some particular passage again on your own, or ask a mature believer.

6. Have you noticed any areas (thoughts, attitudes, behavior) in which you have changed as a result of studying Hebrews? If so, how have you changed?

_____

_____

_____

_____

_____

_____

_____

179

For Further Study: If you have not already done so, you might want to try putting together your own outline of Hebrews. Even an abbreviated one will help you retain what you have learned.

a. First, assign a title to the whole book.

b. At the top of your paper, summarize in a short sentence what you think the book's main purpose is.

c. Give a title to each of the main sections of the book (the Table of Contents of this study guide breaks the book into main sections).

d. Fill in as many supporting sections as you need.

7. Look back over the study at questions in which you planned some specific application. Are you satisfied with your follow-through? What areas continue to challenge you to further attention, and what do you plan to do about them?

_____

_____

_____

_____

_____

_____

For the group

Questions. In order to allow plenty of time to share answers to questions 6 and 7, you will probably have to select just a few of the topics in questions 2 and 3 for discussion.

Be sure to let anyone ask any questions he or she still has about the book. Try to let the group answer all questions raised, or suggest ways of finding answers.

Evaluation. Consider taking a few minutes, or even a whole meeting, to evaluate how your group functioned during your study of Hebrews. Some questions you might ask are:

How well did the study help you grasp Hebrews?
What did you like best about your meetings?
What did you like least? What would you change?
How well did you meet the goals you set at your first meeting?
What did you learn about small group study?
What are members' current needs? What will you do next?

Prayer. Thank God for what He has taught you and how He has been changing you through your study of Hebrews. Ask Him to continue to work on each of you in the areas you have named.

STUDY AIDS

For further information on the material in this study, consider the following sources. If your local bookstore does not have them, you can have the bookstore order them from the publisher, or you can find them in most seminary libraries. Many university and public libraries also carry these books.

Commentaries on Hebrews

Bruce, F.F. *The Epistle to the Hebrews* (New International Commentary on the New Testament, Eerdmans, 1979).
    An outstanding and accurate commentary. Excellent footnotes, and a valuable section entitled, "Argument of the Epistle to the Hebrews," which summarizes the message of the letter.

Griffith-Thomas, W.H. *Hebrews: A Devotional Commentary* (Eerdmans, 1970).
    A collection of forty-one devotional messages based on the theme of Hebrews. Griffith-Thomas continually stresses the importance of spiritual progress in the Christian life. This book is not for in-depth study, but it will prompt devotion and application.

Hodges, Zane C. "Hebrews," *The Bible Knowledge Commentary* (Victor Books, 1983).
    An excellent, very conservative, and brief exposition of the book.

Hughs, Philip Edgecumbe. *A Commentary on the Epistle to the Hebrews* (Eerdmans, 1977).
    A capable exposition, especially helpful for historical background.

MacArthur, John F. *The MacArthur New Testament Commentary: Hebrews* (Moody Press, 1983).

A helpful introduction to Hebrews with rich word studies sprinkled throughout. Easy to read, and good for historical background, cross-references, and applications for modern Christians.

Newell, William R. *Hebrews: Verse by Verse* (Moody Press, 1947).
Although Newell is primarily expositing the book's meaning, he also pays a great deal of attention to the devotional aspects of Hebrews.

Historical and Background Sources

Bruce, F. F. *New Testament History* (Doubleday, 1980).
A readable history of Herodian kings, Roman governors, philosophical schools, Jewish sects, Jesus, the early Jerusalem church, Paul, and early gentile Christianity. Well-documented with footnotes for the serious student, but the notes do not intrude.

Harrison, E. F. *Introduction to the New Testament* (Eerdmans, 1971).
History from Alexander the Great—who made Greek culture dominant in the biblical world—through philosophies, pagan and Jewish religion, Jesus' ministry and teaching (the weakest section), and the spread of Christianity. Very good maps and photographs of the land, art, and architecture of New Testament times.

Packer, James I., Merrill C. Tenney, William White, Jr. *The Bible Almanac* (Thomas Nelson, 1980).
One of the most accessible handbooks of the people of the Bible and how they lived. Lots of photos and illustrations liven an already readable text.

Concordances, Dictionaries, and Handbooks

A *concordance* lists words of the Bible alphabetically along with each verse in which the word appears. It lets you do your own word studies. An *exhaustive* concordance lists every word used in a given translation, while an *abridged* or *complete* concordance omits either some words, some occurrences of the word, or both.

The two best exhaustive concordances are *Strong's Exhaustive Concordance* and *Young's Analytical Concordance to the Bible*. Both are available based on the King James Version of the Bible and the New American Standard Bible. *Strong's* has an index by which you can find out which Greek or Hebrew word is used in a given English verse. *Young's* breaks up each English word it translates. However, neither concordance requires knowledge of the original language.

Among other good, less expensive concordances, *Cruden's Complete Concordance* is keyed to the King James and Revised Versions, and *The NIV Complete Concordance* is keyed to the New International Version. These include all references to every word included, but they omit "minor" words. They also lack indexes to the original languages.

A **Bible dictionary** or **Bible encyclopedia** alphabetically lists articles about people, places, doctrines, important words, customs, and geography of the Bible.

The New Bible Dictionary, edited by J. D. Douglas, F. F. Bruce, J. I. Packer, N. Hillyer, D. Guthrie, A. R. Millard, and D. J. Wiseman (Tyndale, 1982) is more comprehensive than most dictionaries. Its 1300 pages include quantities of information along with excellent maps, charts, diagrams, and an index for cross-referencing.

Unger's Bible Dictionary by Merrill F. Unger (Moody, 1979) is equally good and is available in an inexpensive paperback edition.

The Zondervan Pictorial Encyclopedia edited by Merrill C. Tenney (Zondervan, 1975, 1976) is excellent and exhaustive, and is being revised and updated in the 1980's. However, its five 1000-page volumes are a financial investment, so all but very serious students may prefer to use it at a church, public, college, or seminary library.

Unlike a Bible dictionary in the above sense, *Vine's Expository Dictionary of New Testament Words* by W. E. Vine (various publishers) alphabetically lists major words used in the King James Version and defines each New Testament Greek word that KJV translates with that English word. *Vine's* lists verse references where that Greek word appears, so that you can do your own cross-references and word studies without knowing any Greek.

Vine's is a good basic book for beginners, but it is much less complete than other Greek helps for English speakers. More serious students might prefer *The New International Dictionary of New Testament Theology*, edited by Colin Brown (Zondervan) or *The Theological Dictionary of the New Testament* by Gerhard Kittel and Gerhard Friedrich, abridged in one volume by Geoffrey W. Bromiley (Eerdmans).

A **Bible atlas** can be a great aid to understanding what is going on in a book of the Bible and how geography affected events. Here are a few good choices:

The Macmillan Atlas by Yohanan Aharoni and Michael Avi-Yonah (Macmillan, 1968, 1977) contains 264 maps, 89 photos, and 12 graphics. The many maps of individual events portray battles, movements of people, and changing boundaries in detail.

The New Bible Atlas by J. J. Bimson and J. P. Kane (Tyndale, 1985) has 73 maps, 34 photos, and 34 graphics. Its evangelical perspective, concise and helpful text, and excellent research make it a very good choice, but its greatest strength is its outstanding graphics, such as cross-sections of the Dead Sea.

The Bible Mapbook by Simon Jenkins (Lion, 1984) is much shorter and less expensive than most other atlases, so it offers a good first taste of the usefulness of maps. It contains 91 simple maps, very little text, and 20 graphics. Some of the graphics are computer-generated and intriguing.

The Moody Atlas of Bible Lands by Barry J. Beitzel (Moody, 1984) is scholarly, very evangelical, and full of theological text, indexes, and references. This admirable refrence work will be too deep and costly for some, but Beitzel shows vividly how God prepared the land of Israel perfectly for the acts of salvation He was going to acomplish in it.

A *handbook* of biblical customs can also be useful. Some good ones are *Today's Handbook of Bible Times and Customs* by William L. Coleman (Bethany, 1984) and the less detailed *Daily Life in Bible Times* (Nelson, 1982).

For Small Group Leaders

The Small Group Leader's Handbook by Steve Barker et al. (InterVarsity, 1982). Written by an InterVarsity small group with college students primarily in mind. It includes information on small group dynamics and how to lead in light of them, and many ideas for worship, building community, and outreach. It has a good chapter on doing inductive Bible study.

Getting Together: A Guide for Good Groups by Em Griffin (InterVarsity, 1982). Applies to all kinds of groups, not just Bible studies. From his own experience, Griffin draws deep insights into why people join groups; how people relate to each other; and principles of leadership, decision making, and discussions. It is fun to read, but its 229 pages will take more time than the above book.

You Can Start a Bible Study Group by Gladys Hunt (Harold Shaw, 1984). Builds on Hunt's thirty years of experience leading groups. This book is wonderfully focused on God's enabling. It is both clear and applicable for Bible study groups of all kinds.

How to Build a Small Groups Ministry by Neal F. McBride (NavPress, 1994). This hands-on workbook for pastors and lay leaders includes everything you need to know to develop a plan that fits your unique church. Through basic principles, case studies, and worksheets, McBride leads you through twelve logical steps for organizing and administering a small groups ministry.

How to Lead Small Groups by Neal F. McBride (NavPress, 1990). Covers leadership skills for all kinds of small groups—Bible study, fellowship, task, and support groups. Filled with step-by-step guidance and practical exercises to help you grasp the critical aspects of small group leadership and dynamics.

DJ Plus, a special section in *Discipleship Journal* (NavPress, bimonthly). Unique. Three pages of this feature are packed with practical ideas for small groups. Writers discuss what they are currently doing as small group members and leaders. To subscribe, write to Subscription Services, Post Office Box 54470, Boulder, Colorado 80323-4470.

Bible Study Methods

Braga, James. *How to Study the Bible* (Multnomah, 1982).
    Clear chapters on a variety of approaches to Bible study: synthetic, geographical, cultural, historical, doctrinal, practical, and so on. Designed to help the ordinary person without seminary training to use these approaches.

Fee, Gordon, and Douglas Stuart. *How to Read the Bible For All Its Worth* (Zondervan, 1982).
    After explaining in general what interpretation (exegesis) and application (hermneneutics) are, Fee and Stuart offer chapters on interpreting and applying the different kinds of writing in the Bible: Epistles, Gospels, Old Testament Law, Old Testament narrative, the Prophets, Psalms, Wisdom, and Revelation. Fee and Stuart also suggest good commentaries on each biblical book. They write as evangelical scholars who personally recognize Scripture as God's Word for their daily lives.

Jensen, Irving L. *Independent Bible Study* (Moody, 1963), and *Enjoy Your Bible* (Moody, 1962).
    The former is a comprehensive introduction to the inductive Bible study method, especially the use of synthetic charts. The latter is a simpler introduction to the subject.

Wald, Oletta. *The Joy of Discovery in Bible Study* (Augsburg, 1975).
    Wald focuses on issues such as how to observe all that is in a text, how to ask questions of a text, how to use grammar and passage structure to see the writer's point, and so on. Very helpful on these subjects.

Titles in the LifeChange series:

BIBLE STUDIES AND SMALL-GROUP MATERIALS FROM NAVPRESS

BIBLE STUDY SERIES
Design for Discipleship
Foundation for Christian Living
God in You
Learning to Love
The Life and Ministry of
    Jesus Christ
LifeChange
Love One Another
Pilgrimage Guides
Radical Relationships
Studies in Christian Living
Thinking Through Discipleship

TOPICAL BIBLE STUDIES
Becoming a Woman of Excellence
Becoming a Woman of Freedom
Becoming a Woman of Prayer
Becoming a Woman of Purpose
The Blessing Study Guide
Celebrating Life!
Growing in Christ
Growing Strong in God's Family
Homemaking
Husbands and Wives
Intimacy with God
Jesus Cares for Women
Jesus Changes Women
Lessons on Assurance
Lessons on Christian Living
Loving Your Husband
Loving Your Wife
A Mother's Legacy
Parents and Children
Praying from God's Heart
Strategies for a Successful
    Marriage
Surviving Life in the Fast Lane
To Run and Not Grow Tired
To Stand and Not Be Moved
To Walk and Not Grow Weary

What God Does When Men Pray
When the Squeeze is On

**BIBLE STUDIES WITH
COMPANION BOOKS**
Bold Love
Daughters of Eve
The Discipline of Grace
The Feminine Journey
From Bondage to Bonding
Hiding from Love
Inside Out
The Practice of Godliness
The Pursuit of Holiness
Secret Longings of the Heart
Spiritual Disciplines for the
    Christian Life
Tame Your Fears
Transforming Grace
Trusting God
What Makes a Man?

SMALL-GROUP RESOURCES
201 Great Questions
Discipleship Journal's 101 Best
    Small-Group Ideas
How to Build a Small-Groups
    Ministry
How to Have Great Small-Group
    Meetings
How to Lead Small Groups
The Navigator Bible Studies
    Handbook
New Testament LessonMaker
The Small-Group Leaders
    Training Course

NAVPRESS ◑
BRINGING TRUTH TO LIFE
www.navpress.com